# Learning to BE

"We live in a hectic world and if we are not careful, our faith will become just one more thing on our to-do list. This is a book that so many of us have been waiting for. With historic wisdom and a practical insight, Chad invites us on a spiritual pilgrimage to slow down, step back in time, and rediscover the blessings that come from practicing spiritual disciplines in our daily life."

—**Rev. Dr. Winfield Bevins**, Director of Church Planting at Asbury Seminary and Author of *Ever Ancient Ever New: The Allure of Liturgy for a New Generation*

"Chad's experience and heart help to illuminate the insightful pages of *Learning to Be*. He identifies some of the spiritual toxins in our culture and curates some healthy ways forward. We so need this today. Fr. Chad offers some wise soul-care. I'm excited for you to read this work."

— **Jeremy Cowart**, Photographer and Founder of The Purpose Hotel

"Chad Jarnagin is making a meaningful contribution to the growing importance and awareness of spiritual health. *Learning to Be* is a wise, essential, and helpful book. There is a level of self-awareness and care revealed in Fr. Chad's messaging. The contemplative pace and insight of *Learning to Be* may be just what you need."

— **Ian Morgan Cron**, Author of *The Road Back to You*

"Chad is one of the most profound spiritual leaders I've ever met. *Learning to Be* may just be the most pleasant surprise I have read in a long time. I am grateful to know Fr. Chad and I trust his heart and soul-care. He has a way of making us think and slow down. This book is a gift."

— **Jeff Goins**, Bestseller Author of *Real Artists Don't Starve*

"In *Learning to Be*, Chad Jarnagin is our tour guide to an inspired, reimagined, and winsome journey of faith. For so many of us who feel increasingly out of place in a polarizing and political evangelicalism, Chad helps us to discover new gold from ancient Christian practices—rooting us in a tradition that is deep and wide. If you are ready to trade the muchness and manyness of Christianity for simplicity and stillness, *Learning to Be* provides a much-needed map."

— **Hunter Mobley**, Enneagram Teacher and Pastor at Christ Church Nashville

"So grateful to see someone voicing some of the tensions with embracing wonder and mystery in a culture obsessed with certainty. Fr. Chad lovingly walks us through *Learning to Be* with care and wisdom. He voices how we are human beings, not human doings, something I'm still learning. Thankfully, Chad raises awareness that knowledge and formation leads us toward practice and transformation. I am resonating with this book on my path of learning to be."

— **Harris, III**, Illusionist & Storyteller

"I've had the gift and privilege of friendship with Fr. Chad for several years and I'm excited for others to experience his voice as I have, which is the voice of a wise guide helping us on our spiritual journey. *Learning to Be* is full of practical wisdom encouraging us to keep going and to stay connected to each other and the Ancient Wisdom of the slow work God."

— **Stu Garrard**, Author, Musician, Collaborator,
The Beatitudes Project

"This book is a treasure calling us into stillness, awareness and a deeper communion with our God and with our fellow pilgrims on this spiritual quest. Fr. Chad introduces us to practices that will still our hearts, increase our wonder and draw us into the presence of the living God—the I AM. It calls us forward by inviting us to discover the ancient traditions of faith and to make them our own."

— **Karen Pascal**, Executive Director,
Henri Nouwen Society

"*Learning to Be* is an important read on the path to spiritual health, and Chad is a trusted guide. He not only helps us to courageously name what no longer brings life, but he wisely and graciously points us toward a way forward. If you are looking to reconstruct after the deconstruction, I recommend this book."

— **Aaron Niequist**, Author of *The Eternal Current*

Learning to

# BE

*Reconstructing
Peace &
Spiritual Health*

Chad E. Jarnagin

NASHVILLE

NEW YORK • LONDON • MELBOURNE • VANCOUVER

# Learning to BE
## *Reconstructing Peace & Spiritual Health*

© 2019 Chad E. Jarnagin

Published in New York, New York, by Morgan James Publishing. Morgan James is a trademark of Morgan James, LLC. www.MorganJamesPublishing.com

ISBN 978-1-64279-524-0 paperback
ISBN 978-1-64279-525-7 eBook
Library of Congress Control Number: 2019936245

**Cover Design by:**
Rachel Lopez
www.r2cdesign.com

**Interior Design by:**
Bonnie Bushman
The Whole Caboodle Graphic Design

In an effort to support local communities, raise awareness and funds, Morgan James Publishing donates a percentage of all book sales for the life of each book to Habitat for Humanity Peninsula and Greater Williamsburg.

Get involved today! Visit
www.MorganJamesBuilds.com

# Table of Contents

# Acknowledgements

*Don't let me ever think, dear God, that I was anything but the instrument for Your story.*

**—Flannery O'Connor**

To my beautiful wife, Jennifer. Thank you for not only tolerating my tangents but supporting them. You remind me of the love of the Savior on a daily basis.

To Judah, Xavier, and Elijah, I am incredibly proud to be your father and coach. No matter where you go, what you do, who you become, you will always belong to me. I am with you and for you.

My mother, Brenda. You are a bright light to so many. I want to be more like you when I grow up.

Cunninghams, Palermos, Smiths, and family tribes near and far, I am grateful to celebrate the rhythms of life with you all.

The Kickstarter Backers, you all made this first effort a reality. I am grateful, humbled, and honored by your trust and generosity.

Luminous Parish, our orbit is bright. May our Great Light continue to illuminate our hearts. May you know the depths and vastness of Christ's love and presence in the breaking of the bread.

Thomas Keating, whose life expired during the time I was writing this work. Fr. Thomas will be a light to us all for generations to come.

Mary Oliver, another light who parted from us during the writing of this work. May her words illuminate many hearts.

Nashville, slow your growth or provide mass transit to sustain your expansiveness, please.

To all those who stand and work for justice around the world, your work, our work is a holy one. Grace, mercy, and peace be yours.

To the glory of the Father, and of the Son, and of the Holy Spirit. As it was in the beginning, is now, and will be forever. Amen.

# Introduction

*Our desire to be successful, well liked, and influential becomes increasingly less important as we move closer to God's heart. To our surprise, we even may experience a strange inner freedom to follow a new call or direction as previous concerns move into the background of our consciousness.*

—*Henri Nouwen*

Since the mid 1990s, I have had the privilege of writing, speaking, singing, and touring. As a young child, I found joy and solace in baseball, music, and even philosophy. There were years where I had a great deal of outside influence on my spirituality. In my twenties, I found myself gravitating to liturgy and reverent means to devotion, but there was something odd about my reality; I didn't practice my faith in those kinds of environments. It wasn't until I moved to Nashville where I found my home in an Episcopal church, only to be wooed into a large evangelical church where I began serving middle and high school students. After time went on, I *graduated* to the "big church."

After several years of drifting out on Wednesdays in time for noon eucharist at a nearby historic Episcopal church, I began what seemed to be my second round of deconstructing my faith. Over time, I began to be aware of many others doing the same. If there is strength in numbers, we are all in good company.

Nothing unites or divides quite like our thoughts and opinions on life. There are complexities and variables to our biases, experiences, prejudices, and points of view. Society is a blend of toxic and non-toxic people. We are healthy and unhealthy, joyous and depressed. Traditionally, we gravitate toward those with whom and the things in which we resonate most deeply.

I don't recall being around the Church very often during my upbringing, though I know we went from time to time. What I do remember is that I would have rather stayed home to watch my beloved Cincinnati Bengals or Reds on the TV. As I began to form an awareness of spiritual life, I slowly began to realize that church participation was either helpful for the devoted or problematic for the obligated. The truth that I have come to reluctantly admit is that it can be both.

Over the past decade, I've often pondered: have we justified the erroneous behavior of people within the church walls? Do we actually believe that church activity would camouflage hypocrisy and dark sides forever? In reality, that veil is getting thinner and thinner. People cannot hide from within the church walls any longer under a cloak of invisibility, nor should we. Light will eventually come to the darkness of our life.

The terms "exvangelical" and "post-evangelical" are fitting descriptions for an overwhelming number of people. The terms are identifiers for those who once openly identified themselves as evangelical and now do not. The cause of the exit is more nuanced than political or social. Projecting that one must perform Christian duties in a specific way or have a default worldview on topics such as immigration and healthcare will prove to be problematic. The divisive tension that continues to elevate is exhausting. We can no longer draw clean lines between political parties or social worldviews. Generally, many who follow Jesus interpret the Gospel in different ways through the lens of convenience and preference. Does this resonate?

Our unsustainable pace of life brings fatigue, anxiety, and extraneous stress. Life can provide continual opportunities for perspective. Whenever we have a sense of scale, perspective seems to bring a healthy grounding. During a time where everything is expected to be expedited and instantaneous, it is possible that the modern church has even fallen prey to this unhealthy way of life—leaving many of us disoriented and untethered.

In our efforts to deconstruct our faith, we can be tempted or lulled into a deconstruction that becomes our destination instead of a continual patient process. After all, deconstruction without reconstruction can be destruction. Think of deconstructing faith by dismantling the framework and substance of our theology. Taking it apart from the outside and eventually getting to the inside, an *undoing* and *unknowing* that leads to a *doing* and *new knowing*. Akin to an engine or transmission being taken apart to see if it needs adjustments or repair. Much like the trauma we experience in life, it will affect where we go and what we do going forward. Many of us hold too tightly to the harm, injustice, or pain we have experienced. "The Way" forward will be long, patient, daunting, but hopefully, healing and liberating.

Life is a process of deconstruction and reconstruction, or perhaps you would rather see it as retraction and expansion. Whatever your approach, it will not be a one-time process. I know several people who are on their second or third round of undoing and unknowing as well as a few who are now reconstructing or reframing again (doing and new knowing). Our *knowing* should patiently lean us toward an embodiment. We must remember we are human beings, not human doings. There is a void of peace, wonder, and spiritual health in our divided humanity. We hurt, we bleed, yes, but we can also begin to recover, heal, and move forward. The way forward may actually be to embrace our brokenness and resolve to believe that life may never be fully resolved.

More than likely you will find that any meaningful insights that may resonate have been derived by many who have gone before us. Every day a new book is released about "hacking your way through life," a "shortcut for your success and fulfillment," or some version of how to make more money by working less.

The process of spiritual formation cannot be expedited. In fact, shortcuts can lead to spiritual deformation. Fast tracking any level of discipleship doesn't allow for the best retention or application. We wouldn't place someone who had played soccer their entire life onto a baseball team if they knew nothing of the game. They have to at least know the goal of some of the framework of the game, so they have an idea of how to contribute. A deeper imprint occurs from an immersed existence.

Our great feast is beautiful and savory; we mustn't lessen it to a drive-thru cheeseburger. Our faith is ancient, deep, and weighty. Benedictine spirituality, as we will discuss in more detail later on, would say life is a process of falling down and getting back up again.

Sacred rhythms help us make sense out of chaos, as well as sense God differently. We must intentionally fight for margin in life so we can navigate the demands, noise, and pace that fatigue us. These demands represent a malnourishment or deformation to which all of us have been subjected. Being able to navigate doesn't mean to be unaffected by circumstances. It doesn't mean we are unaware or indifferent to our responsibilities more than meaning we must set boundaries. Boundaries are healthy, needed, and of utmost importance if we are to be productive, balanced, and engaged in our respected lives. Think of it as attempting to sprint for miles vs. running a steady and sustainable pace without wearing ourselves out too quickly.

When wonder and curiosity are less valued, if not dismissed entirely, we can recognize that we may be unhealthy or unbalanced. Mystery and paradox will potentially confuse, frustrate, and even fray our faith rather than inspire it. However, when we are healthy, our need to control aspects of our life diminishes and our faith actually begins to deepen. When our faith begins to deepen, we become the best of our true selves. We will sense the "otherness" found in mystery, which will inevitably lead us toward more awareness and communion with *I AM*[1] as well as one another.

Many of us have a very reduced concept of God, or we have a distorted idea of who God may or may not be. *I AM* is present to us, but we are no longer present to *I AM*, because we are no longer contemplative. The moment God is "figured out" with nice, neat lines and definitions, we're no longer dealing with God. Anne Lamott says, "You can safely assume you've created God in your own image when it turns out that God hates all the same people you do."[2]

When parts of the body are removed (or remove themselves), they eventually wither from a lack of nutrients and koinonia (communion). This separation hinders the part and the whole. When tempted to unravel things of faith and spirituality in isolation, find a safe place to do so around others who care for your well-being.

Unfortunately, we add unneeded pressures to our already turbulent lives. Christians are not exempt. It will serve us well to remember that we are responsible to the Gospel, not for the Gospel. We may need to recognize an unofficial sacrament, the Sacrament of Silence. Silence is a companion of mystery, and the listening is its fellow traveler. A central statement of Judaism

1    Exodus 3:14 (ESV)
2    Anne Lamott, *Bird by Bird* (Anchor Books, 1995), 22.

is the Shema prayer, "Hear, O Israel." So, Israel is a listening people; when it does not listen, and it ceases to be Israel because it falls out of Covenant.

*A moment of insight is a fortune, transporting us beyond the confines of measured time.*
**—Abraham Joshua Heschel**

There is no reconstruction without movement. Movement is misdirected without our ability to listen. It is as if there is a *rebirth*, *reknowing*, or *reformation* that occurs. To proceed toward healthy spirituality, we eventually move into a phase of reconstruction. The sacred text seems to compel those who give space to slowing down, listening, and stillness. Throughout history, the space and posture where God is presently calling us for deeper communion isn't typically a part of popular culture. (Romans 12:2, 1 Peter 2:9, John 17:15–18, 1 Cor. 6:19). May we pay attention to the tension.

Throughout the book, I encourage you to pause at each section for some moments of stillness and silence. Postures are incredibly important. Our particular positioning or approach adjusts our reception, attention, and attitude. Meaning, a certain type of posture will either enable or disable our intention in any context. They will enable a deeper level of awareness, retention, and will intentionally slow your pace. You may become surprised by how resilient the object of your faith is making you.

As a beginning posture, I submit an ancient prayer called the Collect for Purity, or prayer of purity. This century's old prayer has been a centering prayer for millions throughout the years. It is meant to modify our approach as we move ahead. The Collect echoes David's Psalm 51:10 and gives us an intentional approach to a potential reknowing, or relearning.

> *Almighty God, to you all hearts are open, all desires known, and from you no secrets are hid. Cleanse the thoughts of our hearts by the inspiration of your Holy Spirit, that we may perfectly (wholly) love you, and worthily magnify your holy Name through Christ our Lord. Amen.*[3]

---

3   *The Book of Common Prayer* (Cambridge: Cambridge University Press), 237.

## Section I
# PAY ATTENTION

**Please consider practicing one minute of complete silence.**

*Instructions for living a life: Pay attention. Be astonished.*
*Tell about it.*

**—Mary Oliver**

*Chapter One*
# Life is a Pilgrimage

*Spiritual identity means we are not what we do or what people say about us. And we are not what we have. We are the beloved daughters and sons of God.*
**—Henri Nouwen**

We don't use the term pilgrimage very often, and for good reason. It is usually mentioned to describe long journeys of spiritual significance. Do you remember your first time to travel? What do you remember about it? Chances are your recollection isn't entirely accurate. Our expectations inform our memories over time and leave us with an idea of what we want to remember. Managing our expectations is no easy feat. It requires an abundance of energy. Quite frankly, an undoing of our expectations would serve us well, especially when it comes to our spiritual life and health.

Henry David Thoreau, a great explorer once wrote in his journal, "It matters not where or how far you travel—the farther commonly the worse—but how much alive you are."[4] Our level of aliveness probably depends on experiences and how we have responded to them. Life's tragedies can wound us on deep levels, leaving us fractured and traumatized.

Unfortunately, the church has been a "culprit" of harm as well. On our own, we can be hopelessly battered. If we can overcome the darkness to sense and acknowledge the Light that is here to heal and restore, we will begin to return to the Love who wants nothing less than a holy communion with His children. Even though we bring our baggage to every relationship, even a holy one, we are encouraged to come as we are... only to eventually leave it at the very point we can no longer carry it... in reality, it has already been discarded on our behalf.

Through the guidance of the Holy Spirit, we have a deep and constant communion with God, enabling his "Kingdom Come" and his will being done on earth as it is in heaven. Communion goes beyond an intimate interaction or connection; it is a deepening embodiment of the Lord's Prayer. *Our Father, who art in Heaven, hallowed be thy name; thy kingdom come, thy* will *be done, on earth as it is in Heaven. Give us this day our daily bread; and forgive us our trespasses as we forgive those who*

4     Henry David Thoreau, *The Journal of Henry David Thoreau, 1837–1861* (NYRB Classics; Original edition, November 24, 2009).

*trespass against us; and lead us not into temptation but deliver us from evil.[5] For thine is the kingdom, and the power, and the glory, forever. Amen.*

> *First, we must call people to communion with God, to intimacy with God, to a sense of belonging. Most people are lost, confused, alienated. They suffer and struggle immensely in relationships. We have to proclaim loudly and clearly in our actions and in our words that God loves us that we belong to him. That's a call to the mystical life.*
> **—Henri Nouwen**

The development of habits and rhythms, which everyone can acquire, will be both positive and negative. There are healthy habits and rhythms as well as unhealthy habits and rhythms. Change is inevitable. Growth is intentional. Growth and progress will naturally come from healthy and intentional practices and rhythms, much like a continual tuning of a musical instrument. To find rhythm means to intentionally develop patterns for one's enjoyment, health, and well-being. We have patterns of waking, eating, living, and going to sleep. Our bodies and souls are intertwined— when one is unhealthy, it affects the other. Healthy rhythms, sacred rhythms, tend to an inner pattern of communion, and spiritual, mental, and emotional health. Intentionality leads to implementation.

---

5   Matthew 6:9–13 (ESV)

*Growth is not merely a harmonious increase in size, but a transformation.*

**—Maria Montessori**

Human beings may not always get along, but the fact is, it seems that we can't get enough of one another. There are currently more than seven billion of us in the world, but we inhabit only about 10 percent of the planet's land, and roughly 50 percent of us live on just 1 percent of that land.

From the beginning, we were meant to ingest, discuss, and translate Scripture, theology, and ideas together in community. Learning and processing in isolation can be difficult, problematic, or even dangerous. Light and life cannot fully live in a vacuum. Within an active culture of individualized faith practice, our isolation creates an absence of balance, health, and community. Basically, we're better together. Trust requires patience, time, and investment, and trust leads to true community, understanding, and civility.

Many people have an image of God that keeps them in continual anxiety. Henry Guntrip, a British psychoanalyst, notes: *It is a common experience in psychotherapy to find patients who fear and hate God, a God who, in the words of J.S. Mackenzie, "is always snooping around after sinners," and who "becomes an outsize of the threatening parent... The child grows up fearing evil rather than loving good; afraid of vice rather than in love with virtue."*[6]

---

6    Henry Guntrip, *Psychotherapy and Religion* (Harper & Bros., 1957), 194.

A lack of control is often what enables us to let go. Profound movement happens in the lives of undone humans. When we come to the end of ourselves, we begin to see there is finally space for I AM, which moves us to the feasting of good, healthy, and holy things.

> *Healing our image of God heals the image of ourselves.*
> **—Brennan Manning**

I've found myself in many different types of church circles. I could write a book about my decades of touring. One story comes to mind; I believe this occurred somewhere in Virginia. I recall getting out of the bus to begin to set up the band gear, only to find all the church doors were locked. You constantly have to stay on point with your details when traveling from city to city. Sometimes you even mix up your time zones.

Once we looked at the details of load-in time and made a few calls, everything checked out. Yet, no one was there. We waited close to an hour before anyone showed up. Any time something like this happens, it begins to raise flags. When someone finally arrived to unlock the doors, the flags continued to rise. One strange thing after another. Thirty minutes before we were to begin, we still hadn't met with any level of leadership at the church. I looked at the other guys in the band and said, "This is strange for a reason. Meaning, this isn't going to be a normal night, so let's just go with it and pay attention to the vibe and see where things go."

The room became fairly full of mostly normal-looking families of all ages. When it was time to start, we were still waiting to speak with anyone who seemed to be in charge. All of a sudden, the doors opened and at least eight men walked through. We stared in curious disbelief. These men, including the "senior pastor," walked in to the applause of the people. I was confused, irritated, amused, and horrified all at the same time. "What is happening?" was my singular thought at the moment. We found ourselves in the middle of a "Christian" cult group where the main pastor and his council were elevated to a place of worship and adoration.

Over the years, I have come to find that an alarming number of evangelical churches do just that, though a bit more on a subversive level. If life is a pilgrimage, being watchers of the famous becomes a distraction of our true journey. When we allow our attraction to celebrity-like personalities to be formed into the main focal point of our churches, it is no longer Christ-centric.

More often than not, we become by-products of our environments. A friend of mine once said, "This is your life, these are the terms, now what is the invitation?" When examining or assessing your reality, it is helpful to reflect on this. Much like a beautiful hike in the Great Smoky Mountains, it serves you well to stop and take in the view to fully appreciate the experience. Observing a thousand little things will bring about a sense of perspective and rootedness.

May the thirst and communion of contemplation find you willing, available, and open. This contemplation is a gift, not an achievement.

*The great illusion of leadership is to think that man can be led out of the desert by someone who has never been there.*
**—Henri Nouwen**

*Chapter Two*

# Communion >
# Consumerism

S tudies show over 40 percent of American adults suffer from loneliness, a condition that is as dangerous to our physical health as smoking fifteen cigarettes a day.[7] Worse, loneliness is a condition that makes no demographic distinctions; it affects millennials just starting their careers, widowed boomers just ending theirs, Gen Xers, empty-nesters, new divorcees, first-year college students a thousand miles away from family and friends. Social media, which ostensibly draws people closer, in fact may be atomizing us further, creating virtual connections that have little of the benefits of actual connections. Consumerism

---

7    G. Oscar Anderson, "Loneliness Among Older Adults: A National Survey of Adults 45+," https://assets.aarp.org/rgcenter/general/loneliness_2010.pdf, (September 2010).

leads us into a vacuum of individualism and a lessening of communion—communion with one another and with God.

We seem to have evolved to depend on our social connections through the lens of consumer value—what value does it bring to my life? Over thousands of years, this was baked into our nervous systems. We feel socially disconnected, which can place us in a physiologic stress state. We see the effects of this in our everyday life and when viewed in the light of our faith and the Church, we can see that our attraction to consumer life has eroded our life of communion. Once we understand that church is not a singular event, concert, or keynote but rather an incarnate group of people living in community with one another and Christ, we begin to realize it can never be disincarnated. Certainly, we can use modern tools, but we may not call it "church" when it becomes more virtual than communal.

Steven Pressfield, in *The War of Art*[8], discusses the wall of *resistance* that many of us hit while creating. This resistance prohibits many people from pressing into their potential or greatest work. I would suggest that the same can be said of our faith. Many who become disillusioned would do well to sort through the complexities to the core. Their tensions may be with the church or perhaps God, but more probable, the issues may be an individual who represented the church or God. Or perhaps it is the status quo of the constructs that are breaking down. Persevere, dear ones. Once many of us come upon a certain level of resistance or challenge, we tend to retreat or begin attempting alternative routes.

---

8    Steven Pressfield, *The War of Art* (Grand Central Publishing, 2002), 11.

This is a symptom of our lack of catechesis, instructional learning. Catechism is still prevalent in many liturgical churches, however effective, it is intentional. The vast majority of these churches are smaller in nature due to focus, energy, and budget. The parish model has endured for centuries. The modern approach to discipleship has been both the beneficiary and victim of innovation. Technology and innovation can make formative processes more accessible, but we're finding that it may come with a cost.

*The church that can't worship must be entertained.*
**—A.W. Tozer**

The soul damage that has been done and is currently being done in the modern church will be difficult to unravel. Consumerism-Based Faith vs. Communion-Based Faith has been one of the past generation's battles. We've sung "I" and "Me" on Sunday for so long that we've ended up worshiping ourselves. Our communion has been diminished to the points of consumerism, presentation, and preference instead of revelation, repentance, and belonging, not to mention gratitude and devotion.

The Holy Trinity is the concept of God the Father, God the Son, God the Holy Spirit. Unholy trinities may look like "me, myself, and I," "consumerism, nationalism, and individualism," or "my pew, my pastor, my theology." Though for the most part, we may have good intentions, our desires for control, preference, and comfort bear remarkable gravity.

Consumerism from a macro view isn't entirely atrocious, but when we immerse individualism into a subculture, the emphasis of preference exhausts energy while fixating our concentration on our identifiable tribal prejudices. Meaning, anyone who doesn't look, smell, and vote like we do is of lesser importance, while the importance of our singular vantage point is continually elevated above community and common good. An absence of community and connectedness perpetuates and divides, which leads to fear and misunderstandings.

"Rituals and celebrations are signposts to say we live in this time of year, we are in a circle of time; they are ways for people to find their lives connected to the natural flow of life. It is dishonest for anyone to say they don't honor traditions or rhythms. Everyone does at some level. People living outside of the consumer ideology have a different relationship with time. It moves more slowly.

The clock has no meaning to many people living on the margin, or in a subsistence culture or a more traditional society. Being on time is not the point. In west Africa, if the bus shows up within twenty-four hours, it is an on-time departure."[9]

Over time, many have unknowingly viewed activity within the Church as therapeutic. We all certainly need integrated therapy in our daily lives. Integrated therapy is a combined approach to psychotherapy that brings together different or multiple elements of specific therapies. Integrative therapists, for example, may have the view that there is no single approach that can treat each client in all situations. Maybe the Church

9    Peter Block, Walter Brueggemann, and John McKnight, *An Other Kingdom: Departing the Consumer Culture* (Wiley Publishing, 2015).

should be a portion of this integrated therapy, but certainly not exclusively. If it's not, then we may not be doing it properly. Gone are the days where therapy and counseling were only for the broken. Our society is continuing to leave us frayed, fractured, and fatigued. Our heightened self-awareness gives us a sensitivity to our need for wellness.

The depreciation of our memory and ridicule of anything that may seem different from our experience leaves us being problematically judgmental. Many are finding it easier to be entertained instead of disciples. Where I suppose they aren't mutually exclusive, entertainment leaves us malnourished and confused over time. We begin to mistake activity or movement for formation and devotion.

Cognitive-behavioral therapists often ask their patients to write down the critical, debilitating thoughts that make their lives so difficult or frustrating and to practice using different ones. Therapy is frequently one of the only ways forward, and we need our clergy, ministers, and churches to enable healthy rhythms and ways back to spiritual and mental health. Authenticity and transparency cultivate confession, and confession leads to communion. Much of our shame hinders our ability to belong. Belonging can lead to believing. It's okay to not be okay for a time.

For the majority of our lives, regardless of our background, a consumerist approach to faith in life creates environments where you have to believe before you could ever possibly belong. This is extremely problematic for us at some point. Many of us have come to a place in our faith pilgrimage where performance, observation, and the pep rallies no longer suffice.

We are so enamored with our life that we create the idea that all of heaven is sitting around watching us like reality TV, eating popcorn, hanging on our every move. This is faulty and implies that we are the center of the universe on both sides of eternity. It is fair to address the sentiment of being known by our Maker, but wouldn't it be healthier to think about it in a different way? Surely, we aren't suggesting that we are capable of capturing the attention of heaven by our cleverness or activity that would create an inconsequential stir, wooing the gaze of heaven away from the Great Throne.[10] This seems so extravagantly arrogant of us, doesn't it? Throughout Scripture, God's people are called beloved, but our self-centeredness temptation to the be center of the interest of heaven may be an effect of our misguidedness.

Sometimes we need to admit that we simply don't know everything, nor should we. Holding something holy may mean to leave it mysterious. Many folks going to church these days are looking for answers but potentially not the answers our grandparents or even parents were looking for. Many are looking for a place to belong, before they believe. And sometimes they just need some peace and a place to safely exhale. Sometimes, the music can even get in the way of our peace. We don't need more activity, we need more space to be and more space to commune—which is inevitably devotion and worship.

It seems we are too distracted by branding and production preference in the modern church. We have bought into a sort of tribalism that plays to our resemblance, trends, and

---

10    Matthew 23:22, Hebrews 8:1, Revelation 4 (ESV)

inclinations instead of a larger, more diverse communion. Living intentionally may regulate our "busyness" or cluttered schedules. We mustn't confuse activity with accomplishment.

> *There are no unsacred places; there are only sacred places and desecrated places.*
> **—Wendell Berry**

There are some keywords to pay attention to that contribute to the current state of the American church. It may not be exclusively of the American church, but most certainly should be considered—individualism, isolation, and cultural and cognitive dissonance are all complex and complicated factors to navigate. Our state of inconsistent thoughts, beliefs, or attitudes breaks down healthy convictions and decisions. These lead us into much of the cultural and social tensions of today. However, a philosophy of "we" will always be greater than a "me" philosophy. It is curious to realize that when "I" is replaced with "we," the word *illness* becomes *wellness*.

We are obsessed with consuming. We will consume anything at any given time. This may be from our subversive appetite for truth and goodness—but we'll watch the flashy show while believing we are being transformed by its presentation. And yes, this has affected the American church on catastrophic levels. These are observations from experience, conversations, and research. The chase of the spectacle is a symptom of consumerism. Maybe we long for a spectacular moment because we subconsciously want to be distracted from the ordinary. Ironically, there is nothing ordinary about being present in the moment. Reducing God to an elusive event is to reduce the presence of God here, now.

Celebration absent of hype is becoming increasingly more challenging. It's almost like speaking a language that no one understands, though we continue speaking it. The emphasis of individualism not only leaves us breathless, it can leave us soulless and isolated—only left focusing and fixating on our individual circumstances, problems, and ambitions. You can see how this worldview can eventually be problematic.

*People of our time are losing the power of celebration. Instead of celebrating, we seek to be amused or entertained. Celebration is an active state, an act of expressing reverence or appreciation. To be entertained is a passive state—it is to receive pleasure afforded by an amusing act or a spectacle... Celebration is a confrontation, giving attention to the transcendent meaning of one's actions.*
**—Abraham Joshua Heschel**

Evangelicalism is fracturing at an alarming rate and is beyond repair from any high watermark days of previous generations. When churches are known as more of a business where profits and losses are the metrics, they lose the ability to restore, stabilize, and form disciples. There are other ways forward. However, as we go along, we'll discuss some specific distinctions I have come to find helpful, healing, and deeply meaningful.

Performance and production will not sustain our faith. We may even have a misunderstanding of faith. Faith isn't the construct of what we see or have before us. Faith is the remains of our beliefs and certainties, usually found in the ashes of devastation. So, it is quite possible that a consumerist approach to church and faith will only ever be an artificial substitute for wholeness and sustenance.

When branding and user experience become the most illustrious measurables of a church, it is no more a holy place set apart for the devoted than a Jamba Juice at the local mall. When the modern church began to disregard sacramental ways of worship, it may have unknowingly begun its descent into irrelevance, ironically under the blinding pursuit of relevance.

What we do on Sundays at church gatherings does matter. At one point, I couldn't say I believe that. Through the expansion of my heart, mind, and soul, this has changed dramatically over the years. Without a sense of connectedness with the Church around the world, throughout time and dimension (heaven and earth), we can gain a perspective that gives true light and gravity to the Body of Christ, past, present, and future. When we argue that Sunday gatherings don't matter and that only Monday through Saturday is of importance, this may be revealing our individualism and consumerism has become paramount over our communion with I AM and one another.

With our cultivated conveniences, we have begun to rely on technology over communion, a society where our words have become devalued. St. James encouraged people to be slow to speak and quick to listen, but we are slow to listen and quick to speak, and even quicker to anger. Unfortunately, we can be tempted to revel in our discontent.

In our disagreements, we shouldn't retreat from one another. We should lean in. Community doesn't occur easily, nor is it retained easily. Maybe we have become subject to transactional affirmations rather than embodying healthy relationships where trust and respect are fostered. A transaction leads with a potentially misguided motive where an expectation of "gain" is sought. To embody a healthy relationship is to seek a hope of learning through the experience of communion without the expectation of receiving anything in return.

Communion encourages grace, trust, and eventually begins to leave fingerprints on everything it touches, leaving us more beautiful, deeper, enriched, and abounding in empathy. Communion allows us to choose to keep our soul healthy rather than fatigued and consumed.

*Chapter Three*

# Noise

There's a lot of noise in our culture. It's everywhere. From our streets, supermarket, schools, to social media. We now live in a time where everyone can voice their opinion, discontent, frustration, or issues at any given time. There are also opportunities for betterment in this as well. We can now encourage, share insight, inspiration, and ideas openly. Whether we want to admit it or not, we now find ways to compare ourselves to each other with what we perceive with our online personas.

Today's information and expression overload is leaving people looking for some clear certitudes by which to define themselves and others. It seems that there are various forms of fundamentalism in many religious leaders when it serves their cultural or political preference. We surely see it at the lowest levels of religion—Christianity where God is used to justify violence, hatred, prejudice, and whatever our worldview becomes.

The clanging and clutter of our society will take many forms. The dictatorship of noise is subversive in most regards. The rumbles and turbulence of noise ripples throughout our politics, art, academia, and even reaches into our churches.

Years ago, while backstage at an event in Seattle, I was having a conversation with someone from the area. We may have only been conversing for several minutes, but something profound struck me during our time together. The longer we spoke, the louder we began speaking, to the point where we were almost yelling at each other. The background music began to swell and rise to the point where we were physically feeling it. This is fairly normal at concerts.

Before we went on that night, I became aware of something I had never given much thought to. We were about to play for over an hour through a very large and very loud audio system. I should point out that there were two other bands playing an hour prior. Even the music in between the sets were obnoxiously loud. I found myself conflicted before ever going on stage. I wanted to soften the night and wished we were doing a more acoustic set with guitar, keyboards, and cello. Alas, the show went on and we left it all on the stage, or rather left it all on the field for you sports fans.

When we can't even find peace and stillness within a church environment, it may be safe to say that we are doing people a disservice. Our lives are riddled with visual, audible, and social violence. The last thing we need is sonic violence. Have you ever found yourself in a modern worship service while the band is playing, and you continue having a conversation? The music becomes a background soundtrack to your conversation. This white noise can even become an irritation and nuisance. Do you realize that this converts to a deformative energy?

There are many elements that add to the noise and clutter we all sense and feel. Burn-out is constantly on the rise in any genre. We are uncertain on how to bridle and manage life's demands and noise. The progression of technology was supposed to make productivity easier, right? Well, it can when we allow it to work for us rather than hijack our attention, thus adding to the clutter and roar.

Stillness, silence, and meditation help us in seeking space to just *be*. Being is a fully aware and centered state where we acquire peace and rejuvenation. It does not come easy and is anything but passive. A contemplative life is a life that pursues "rest in God," as the *Cloud of Unknowing* mentions. This is a holy rest. Its exhale and breath reach to the deepest parts of us, our soul.[11] We can rest in ways that aren't specifically "holy," but it will not reach the deep parts of our beings. We will sense the Holy in margins of life when given the opportunity. A "selah" can be more of a sacred encounter than any church worship service. We tend to be more kind, gentle, and compassionate when we aren't grasping for control and notoriety due to our urgency to be significant. This isn't an overnight transformation. It's a steady and patient process.

---

11  Author unknown, *The Cloud of Unknowing*.

There is strength in stillness. If we step back from this busy life for a moment of reflection, we will start to hear a deafening silence. The ironic thing will be that it is truly the still silence that is so deafening. Everyone in my circle struggles with noisy, crazy, hectic schedules, running from meeting to meeting, coffee to coffee, and service to service. Being present and available to God through the pursuit of space, focus, and contemplation is something we make difficult for ourselves.

After you read this, just try to take five minutes and sit in silent solitude. This might be hard. No texting, no computer, no music, no iPhone, no gaming, no calls, no talking. Nothing but silence. If you haven't experienced this in a while, the sound will be loud. When we arrive at a place on our journey where we have run out of words to pray, we will find a brilliant presence of God in the stillness, without words.

In a society that breeds narcissism and instant reaction, a true and even disciplined pursuer of the Holy might feel strange or awkward about sitting, kneeling, or laying down. Thoughts of all that we could be doing will attempt to drown out the entire purpose of getting alone to be still, silent, and contemplative. Don't be surprised if your vices, struggles, or addictions reveal themselves. That will be the crossroad choice of what we do with that time. Seek peace or give in to the self-centered nature that we constantly combat.

At some point the Church began to elevate the Pulpit over the Table. It has left many people disoriented, divided, and even deformed. To this day, Christ is and has been known in the breaking of the bread, not a sermon or speech. Our need to communicate and over-communicate may have begun from a proper place to convey the hope and heart of the Gospel, but in many cases, it has begun a descent into a temptation to control, isolate, and even contribute to the noise. This noise is contrary to the peace that is found in our Holy Communion.

A.W. Tozer referred to our experiencing a "breathless silence" when we know God is near. In some instances, absolute silence might be our greatest act of worship.[12] The silence Tozer is talking about doesn't occur in most modern worship gatherings. Everything in our culture is screaming at a decibel level that is dulling our senses. One has to think that our spiritual hearing may become damaged over time. What if the future of the Church could be saturated in moments of stillness, silence, and reverence once again? As we become hungry for this type of silence in our practicing church communities, we will see and sense God in a way where our words would fall short.

*Silence is God's first language; everything else is a bad translation.*
**—Fr. Thomas Keating**

Church leaders would do well to remember that when people come into worship, their life is already fast and loud; church should be more intentionally set apart for rest, peace, healing, and feasting. It can be voluntary or involuntary, but many communities are as fast and loud as a busy restaurant at dinnertime. Our churches are typically no different from anywhere else. How can we lead people into a holy and sacred

---

12   Dick Eastman, *Intercessory Worship* (Chosen Books, 2012), 37.

place if we don't practice and abide in that same space? We can't lead them where we haven't been.

We know that God can and will use broken and busy people but being centered and quiet before Him may open our hearts to hear His heart. When I come into a worship gathering, I *need* the music leaders to help lead me to a place of silencing and yielding of my world in order to seek God. I don't need a cheerleader or noisemaker. We should realize this is all about a balanced approach. High-energy, fist-pumping worship arguably may have its place, if it's honest enthusiasm, but let's not marginalize reverent spaces and contemplation.

Congregants: Practice and develop the art of lingering. Arrive at church a little earlier… leave a little later. When our schedules make us late and pressure us to leave early, we're not mentally or physically present enough to engage. Slow down. Breathe… and intentionally build peace into your life.

I think most of us believe that God is everywhere and in everything to some extent, but how often do we acknowledge that? How do we live in a sacramental and eucharistic way where this belief is embodied? We usually let what is going on in our personal worlds dictate our response to the Almighty. In order to effectively lead people into worship of God, we must be clear to hear where He is leading us.

Application of a true "quiet time" or "silent time" is the only means of execution here. I AM will be in the secret silent place. It probably looks different for everyone; however, we will sense the holiness of the Creator in a unique way. God sees through our pretentious pride and acts, so authenticity should be realized. I AM will draw near to us as we draw near to I AM

(James 4:8). Therein lies the hope to find more frequent time and space to seek, sense, and listen for more of the Creator's heart in the middle of this chaotic life. To neglect our faith is to neglect our souls. At some point some of us turn our faith off because of some traumatic event or some act of hypocrisy that we've experienced.

Fatigue from divisive opinion, passive aggressiveness, and the desire to hustle on social media is pervasive. News cycles and political rhetoric eventually become less problematic for our sanity and peace when we have less of a feed to consume it. When properly curating our social feeds, there will be less noise and chaos visible to us. This is helpful in our self-awareness and soul care.

Our fatigue can affect everything—our capacity for comprehension, objectivity, and even spiritual health. Mental and emotional instability is peaking, and anxiety seems to be inescapable. Let's be attentive to the erosion and warning signs while tending to our self-care. We would do well to be cautious of our fatigue. It can lead us to unlikely places—having less empathy, compassion, and peace can be detrimental to our health, not just mental and emotional health, but relational health. This is already a problem in the church. When we lose our empathy, compassion, and peace, we lose our bearings on how to navigate trauma or turbulence in life, not to mention being enabled to help others navigate life's turbulence.

By lessening our consumption of social media, we lessen the noise in our lives instantaneously. This opens space and opportunity to:

- Seek opportunities to speak with a friend in person.
- Listen and observe.
- Read, retain, and rest.
- Meditate and pray.

One of the most important aspects I would acknowledge during these days would be that I spend more time with others who differ from me. Perspective and healthy discourse is understated today. I am seeking to understand more rather than feeling the need to be understood. I believe the more we open our minds, arms, and tables, the more we actually solidify our worldview. Your worldview should be subject to legitimate challenge to be found worthy of its grounding and conviction. If it is shaken easily, it may need reforming and solidifying.

We are in new days, and we need new light in our lives. I believe we need to be new light to the world of subversive darkness that we combat. We are better together. Curate the relationships closest to you. There may be some that need not be resuscitated. Honor those relationships by letting them go. Fight for those who are worth fighting for. Over the past few years, I've come to terms with the idea of being unfollowed, unfriended, or unsubscribed from. It's not the end. It actually helps you to recalibrate and move forward.

Christ spoke of peace often. To practice peace, we must abide in it. Peace begins in stillness, combatting the noise around us. Once we linger in peace, wear it around our necks, we begin to embody it. Others will sense our peace and will be attracted to it, even if only subversively.

So dear friends, peace be with you, and share peace with everyone you meet.

*Chapter Four*

# The Art of Awareness

There is quite a difference between responding and reacting. First responders are service people who are the first to be called to a scene for emergencies, medical assistance, or law enforcement. They are first responders, not first reactors. When we are subconsciously conditioned to react to events in life, we imitate that type of energy with almost everything else we do. It eventually becomes so unhealthy that we react to false narratives and concepts. Our lack of awareness has many factors, one being our lack of attunement. Attunement with ourselves, one another, and our Creator.

*Certain events, current events, historical events, critical incidents, and life circumstances—serve as signposts*

*pointing to the will of God and the new creation for those
with eyes to see and ears to hear.*
### —Henri Nouwen

Christian thinkers as varied as Soren Kierkegaard, C.S. Lewis, and John Calvin have identified that knowing God and knowing ourselves is personally intertwined, each one supporting and deepening the other.

We are not without a plethora of resources for the process of self-discovery. Our default state of being can become a deep, neurologic groove enabled by our developed habits and patterns in life. Over time many of us wander into anxiety and worry as if we were on autopilot mode. In other words, we don't really cognitively process what we are contemplating. Lowering the noise levels in our brains is an incredible challenge but not a hopeless one. Quieting our mind and soul offers not just a peaceful state, but it opens dimensions of perception where we need it most.

I've always been into personality assessments. I can remember in my early twenties taking my first assessment. I can't even remember what type it was, but I believe it was the Myers-Briggs Type Indicator. I've taken StrengthsFinders (now CliftonStrengths), the DISC, and many others... but it wasn't until the Enneagram that I began to resonate with its messaging and possibilities. If you know anything about the Enneagram, you know that it is proven over centuries and not just a trend.

Personal care begins with space for personal assessment. Self-awareness gives us a deeper awareness of everyone around us. It's a difficult thing for us to process in the stillness, the quiet, but it is incredibly important work. It doesn't take a contemplative person to be in tune with how they are wired; awareness is for everyone.

The Enneagram provides a vast and non-static view of us from the inside out. It does, however, give us a wonderfully well-crafted landscape of who we are, how we are when we're healthy, and who we are when we're stressed.

When shame becomes a stench that we grow accustomed to, it is one of the warning signs that we need a spiritual detox. The process of deconstructing our spiritual life comes with many possible huddles and trappings. Ironically, we can be so wounded by past shame that we continue to carry it around in our pocket like a flask for when we feel a good dose would do us well. That is what detoxing feels like. It feels good at first, then more difficult to let go. Cleansing doesn't happen overnight. We may find that we experience moments of sobriety and epiphany, but it is in the slow, bloody crawl where we begin to find true sustaining change and health.

There are rhythms to our pursuit of health and peace. These rhythms have deeper meanings at their core. We shouldn't allow our modern retention training (or lack of) to affect our knowing and unknowing. *Metanoia* (Greek for "change of mind") is often translated as "repentance" and is the opposite of paranoia. It is a high-minded, higher way of thinking and being. Repentance in English is to say that we have already done something wrong. It is a reduced version of the true meaning of the Greek word *metanoia*.

Our awareness of the here (present) should only transcend to the greater view—that we are only here for a moment in the grand view. All things will and must pass, but God's Kingdom will remain. Our comprehension or level of belief will rise and recede throughout our life, but the need for self-awareness will always linger, and for the betterment of those around us.

*All that you are... every fold and crease of your individuality was devised from all eternity to fit God as a glove fits a hand. All that intimate particularity you can hardly grasp yourself, much less communicate to your fellow creatures, is no mystery to Him. He made those ins and outs that He might fill them.*

**—C.S. Lewis**

*Attunement* and *awareness* are never about the pursuit of perfection. Once you engage the Enneagram, there are immeasurable supplies to the insight and knowledge that we can discover over time. To begin to care for our souls as well as those around us, we must loosen our grip of expectation and control, allowing for the space to discover more of the instruction and wisdom found within the ancient text of Scripture. The more we walk through those pages with a filter of awareness, the more we will begin to comprehend the depth and application of the content. Coincidentally, we will subtly and patiently become less cynical over time. That is just one of the many benefits of becoming healthy. As we continue on the path to peace and spiritual health, we will begin to thirst for less noise and clutter. As an effect of this craving, our attunement and attentiveness will enable us to hear the pulse and voice of our Creator calling us beloved. As Henri Nouwen said, "It is like discovering a well in the desert. Once you have touched wet ground, you want to dig deeper."[13]

> *Perfection is like an ice sculpture: it lasts only as long as there's no change in the atmosphere.*
> **—Suzanne Stabile**

---

13   Henri Nouwen, *Life of the Beloved* (Crossroad Publishing Company), 37.

*Chapter Five*
# Peace and Permission

*To God who rested from all action on the seventh day and*
*ascended upon His throne of glory.*
*He vested the day of rest with beauty;*
*He called the Sabbath a delight.*
*This is the song and the praise of the seventh day, on which*
*God rested from His work.*
*The seventh day itself is uttering praise.*
*A song of the Sabbath day:*
*"It is good to give thanks to the Lord!"*
*Therefore, all the creatures of God bless Him.*[14]

---

14   Abraham Heschel, *The Sabbath* (Farrar Straus Giroux, 2005).

The Sabbath teaches all beings whom to praise. Shalom means "everything in its place, flourishing as God intends."

Every day introduces a new idea, a new way of doing things, and new challenges. "Right brainers" tend to thrive in this era due to the number of channels, mediums, and social implications of being a "creative." For years, I pursued a dangling carrot of creativity and artistry. I thought that if I could introduce the most radical "out of the box" idea, or execute the most outlandish creative moment, then maybe I could receive an award or bonus from the "Cool Kids Creativity Institute." Then I joined the staff at a church, and everything began to change.

Everyone puts contrasting levels of value on creativity. I found myself in a marginalized role. I was to be the token "Bono" on Sundays, bring a good idea to the table here and there, and was expected to just do my job. The expectations were different from what I had set out to pursue.

It didn't take me long to sense that I was doing what I was made to do, and vulnerable to learn more of who I was being compelled to be.

Someone once said to me, "Chad, you might want to stop trying so hard, and just be. Be who you were created to be and not who you think others want you to be." Those words, in addition to how the Spirit was stirring in my life, began to alter my head and heart space. It gave me permission to embrace how I was wired to be. Seeking peace and centeredness through prayer and meditation slowly began to recalibrate my motives, hopes, and ambitions.

Many may think that if you are a priest, pastor, or on staff at a church, you have nothing but time to read, pray, and just soak in the goodness of God… and maybe do some emailing. Though some of those should be a part of who we are (not just what we do), we have demands and expectations projected on us. After some experience, we realize what comes with the "job," and we either embrace the dynamic and do what we can or find another career path.

Fear tends to dictate our actions more than we care to acknowledge. I wonder if we cringe at stillness and silence because of our fear of what we may hear or feel. It is important to contemplate that fear only speaks to those who listen. Fear, biblically, means silent wonder, radical amazement, and affectionate awe at the infinite goodness of God. A wise Irishman, who goes by Bono, once said, "The less we know, the more we can believe." The more experienced I became at producing or crafting an event or experience, the more I began questioning. Questioning everything.

While most modern churches embrace every accessible innovation possible, I began examining the "why" behind what we were doing each week. I began to ponder if just because we can, does that mean we should?

I've been artistic from a very young age. In my mid to late teens, I found myself on all kinds of stages. I even viewed the baseball field as a stage. I began to spread my creative wings with the art form of music, and it took flight. For about twenty-five years, I made a "living" with music, mostly combined with some level of ministry. I was privileged to see much of the world through travel, the stage, and a microphone. I have come to find that obscurity is a blessing. From my years of being in front of people, whether it was 300 or 3,000, the type of person that I defaulted to during this time wasn't the fullness of who I would eventually become. Obscurity brings a peace that allows us time with friends, family, and meaningful work, not to mention a spiritual life of health with space and margin to be a more complete "you."

Life on a stage and in the public eye may sound intriguing, or even fulfilling, until you've experienced it. Quite frankly, I didn't have a successful career in the eyes of the music industry, but I now realize that my work was no less important or enjoyable. Many celebrities are forced to deal with more voices and critics. To have a level of cultural influence will come with tricks and trappings. It becomes increasingly hard to maintain healthy margins and space to be who you need to be off stage. The public would rather you be the same rockstar on and off stage. Anyone with some level of common sense would know that is not possible.

So, everyone (not only the Enneagram "4s"), hear ye when I say, "enjoy the obscurity," for it is a gift.

Several years back, some friends and I created a space to explore and practice contemplation, creativity, and ancient spiritual rhythms. We called it Luminous Project. It became an environment to Converse + Commune + Be. We were hoping for some clarity in our spiritual pilgrimages, in need of encouragement, rest, and authentic conversation. It had to be a creative environment that was safe to unplug from being "on." Basically, we found that we desperately needed ongoing therapy. This gave us permission to ask and discuss some important "why" questions and not just recycle the "how" questions. A great need surfaced. We began to look to our ancient faith's past and learned that this was our way forward.

> *Happiness is not a matter of intensity but of balance, order, rhythm and harmony.*
> **—Thomas Merton**

# Section II
# POSTURES

**Practice five minutes of complete silence.**

*We have to slow down to catch up with God.*
**—N.T. Wright**

*Chapter Six*

# Posture and Practice

In 2012, I traveled to Moldova, the smallest country in the former Soviet Union. It was quite a memorable expedition as we visited three orphanages as well as two Orthodox monasteries. While at the most primitive monasteries I've ever encountered, I was reminded of the beautiful and humbling entry of the prayer chambers. As you enter from the top of a stairwell, your eyes need to adjust to the dimly lit space at the bottom. On your journey downward, you will begin to notice the narrowing of the entrance, gently forcing one to bow upon entry.

I spent some time speaking with members of our group, discussing the ancient and reverent significance of the bowing posture. Many of us would have most certainly recognized this as a holy moment that informed our remaining time there. Our margins were aligned in this space. Maybe it was the weight of the consecration of the abbey or the lives of the monks. There was a heightened sense of peace, restfulness, and simplified beauty.

It didn't take me too long to realize that we have to intentionally contest for margins in life so that we can be unaffected. Being unaffected doesn't mean we are unaware or indifferent to the world around us. It elevates the value of constructing boundaries. Boundaries are healthy, needed, and of utmost importance if we are to be productive, balanced, and engaged in our respected lives.

> *Gratitude's not a natural posture. The prince of darkness is ultimately a spoiled ingrate, and I've spent most of my life as kin to the fist-shaker.*
> **—Ann Voskamp**

The "how" of life should only be addressed once the most important question has been asked. We must ask the "why" question. Without asking the *why* question first, we may be running aimlessly. The slightest of angles can eventually affect the future trajectory. Imagine supporting a political candidate without knowing their position on policies that you had strong convictions. The "why" matters immeasurably. Our meaning of posture is no different. They are the layers in which we align our lifestyle.

Most of the world struggles to find language for traumatic experiences. Betrayal, loneliness, complexity, and crisis force us to process. The awkwardness of finding ourselves around others who are navigating trauma can be telling with how we react or interact. We should be careful and mindful with what we say and how we say it, for we can unintentionally make an already terrible circumstance worse.

To sympathize originally meant "to suffer with." I can recall several conversations with others when my sister died. "Chad, you can never question God's plans, He knows all, and knows what's best." I can neither agree or disagree with the comment on its own. However, we can very much question God in almost any scenario if we are honest. Surely God has capacity for our questions and doubts. I can believe that God does indeed know all. One can move past the content of this comment, but it does reveal the certainty that many of us struggle to find how and what to say during a traumatic situation. Quite frankly, the modern church finds it difficult to identify with suffering.

Sometimes the best thing we can do in these moments is to say nothing at all. Our presence may be the only communication we need to offer. We have a difficult time with shutting up. We love to hear ourselves talk, even if it is nonsense. I would dare say that by attempting to find words to say, we inadvertently belittle some subject matter. Sometimes there simply aren't words for beautiful moments or even traumatic moments. So, anything that is expressed fails to convey the scope of our emotions and thoughts, no matter our intentions.

Have you ever had a friend that you found yourself spending time with where neither of you felt the pressure to continually speak? Those types of friendships are far and few between, but when found it speaks to the depth and understanding in that relationship. There is something beautiful about having the right words to say, but there can be something even more beautiful when we allow the space for silence. It can be a peaceful expression on its own.

I believe we can see the mystery and majesty of God through our broken moments. We don't do ourselves any favors by cheapening moments of deep meaning by saying the wrong thing, not saying the right thing, or saying anything at all. Everything speaks. This applies to normal everyday conversations, worship gatherings, and communication strategies (print, branding, etc.). This may heighten our awareness of the weight found in our words.

There are some significant holy orders that we can reference in our quest for learning and practicing spiritual postures. One specifically stands out in regard to postures. The Rule of St. Benedict is a wonderful monastic way of life. There are several characteristics to Benedictine Spirituality:

- Listening
- Poverty
- Behavior
- Obedience
- Hospitality
- Humility
- Stability
- Balance

It's interesting how many people I come in contact with who are longing for a process from information to transformation but aren't sure where to begin the actual formation. Simply being informed by information isn't enough. Information should lead us further into an embodiment. Like the monastic orders, like Benedictines, embodiment takes intention, devotion, and patience. We must go into the space where information becomes transformative, whatever the context. *Trans*, meaning movement, is formation of information into formative action.

Another monastic posture that assists our reliance and continually softens us is learning to let go. Much of our grasp in life can impede personal growth and health. A lack of control is often what enables us to let go. Profound movement occurs in the lives of the undone. May we be aware that speed is the enemy of depth. A slowing simplification will propagate a healthy intensity to our ever-growing spirituality.

In my years of being a priest / pastor, I've had the privilege of hearing many people's stories. Many of those who have grown up in a Christian environment now attempt to live a life of devotion outside of church involvement. All of us can evaluate how many times we have heard of all the duties and performances required as followers of Jesus. There is an overwhelming anxiety and frustration that begins to creep in and fatigue us from the inside out. These unrealistic expectations can eventually leave us debilitated.

Over time, we may have had someone attempt to interpret Scripture over and over again, telling us we're not doing enough for the Kingdom, that we're not really serious about our faith, or maybe it's because we don't love Jesus enough. After years of hearing similar stories from people I've known, there are resounding tensions with people of The Way. Many have come to just give up, saying "it's just too much, unsustainable, or unhealthy to do all the church asks of us." There are a hundred reasons why many people have left the activities of the church. It's just simply become too much. We are certainly to live selflessly, rather than selfishly, but living in a culture of "doing" only erodes our urgency of "being." When our *doing* comes from a place of genuine posture of devotion, conviction, and *being*, we may finally find ourselves looking like the Church. This is what living with peace and spiritual health begins to look like.

*Chapter Seven*

# A Posture of Pace

Rest and sabbath in a culture of exhaustion may be the only antidote to our soul fatigue. Slowing down our pace of life is becoming more and more difficult. "Taking a deep breath" seems to be a meaningless saying with no frame of reference, though it is one of the first things a therapist or doctor would tell us to do in a stressful situation.

Several years ago, I slowly began to notice specific moments and events that would linger in my memory. These moments were typically found around a table, kitchen island, or fire pit with new and old friends while savoring beverages, food, and conversations. In the words of the talented songwriter Kacey Musgraves: "I'm alright with a slow burn, taking my time, let the world turn."

The word "companion" leads us to the table, originating from the Latin *companionem*, meaning "bread fellow," someone we break bread with. Mary Douglas, a structural anthropologist, imagines social situations as ever decreasing circles that each enclose greater familiarity.[15] We each have concentric circles of intimacy. Who we share our table with also influences what we have as a part of the meal.

We are each wired with specific capacities, desires, and tendencies. We are different, diverse, and unique, which enables and constrains growth and the expansion of our minds. The pace at which we can learn to live over time will either hinder or facilitate growth and health.

Eating is a communal act that allows us to savor the food, converse, and relax. Yet the early 19th century sociologist Georg Simmel argued that cultures put such an emphasis on communal eating because, ultimately, eating alone can confirm our isolation. Finding others who share an interest in slowing their pace of life can sometimes be just as difficult as the act of slowing itself.

> *Why should we be in such a desperate haste to succeed, and in such desperate enterprises? If a man does not keep pace with his companions, perhaps it is because he hears a different drummer. Let him step to the music which he hears, however measured or far away.*
>
> **—Henry David Thoreau**

---

15    Lisa Harris, "Circles of Intimacy," *The Liberal*, http://www.theliberal.
co.uk/artsandculture/harris_circles-of-intimacy.html

Finding pace setters will eventually assist us in slowing ourselves into healthy and mindful postures.

1. Enjoy a beverage that requires sipping versus consuming quickly. The space for conversation and observation will heighten. The noisier an environment, the shorter conversations tend to be. Discover spaces with ambiance. Exhale and enjoy a meaningful and inspiring conversation where listening, speaking, and learning take place.

2. Have a meal where you include others in the process. Converse during the creation as well as the consumption. Resist having every course at the table at once. Take your time. Discuss several subjects. Resist topical conversations that never have the opportunity to get off the ground. Discussing a variety of subjects will enable more meaningful relationships over time.

3. Take the long way home. Drive with the windows down. Music optional.

Slower living may not sound as intriguing to all of us, but it can enable deeper connection with others. Understand that perfectionism is an enemy of pace and communion. I am not just speaking to Enneagram "Ones." The world isn't going to end if the laundry isn't done, if the dishes still aren't loaded, if the children are wearing the wrong shoes, or if you don't complete the to-do list. Jon Kabat-Zinn, a Professor Emeritus at the University of Massachusetts Medical School, once said:

*Mindfulness is a certain way of paying attention that is healing, that is restorative, that is reminding you of who you actually are so that you don't wind up getting entrained into being a human doing rather than a human being.*[16]
— **Jon Kabat-Zinn**

Our questions, frustrations, and uncertainties help us bond with one another. Making some sense of God, faith, and death takes some time and space. Even though almost everything in society is fact / control-oriented, giving one another an intentional pace for conversation is a gift. We tend to get a form of temporary satisfaction from the control, facts, and information we receive. Who likes to be left hanging on the edge of something unresolved? People are afraid of letting go of what they believe they should have control of—emotions, expression, response, and yes… worship. Building mindful relationships with others requires our attention, empathy, and intentional pace.

Your body is a temple and should be respected and cared for. Spending too much time and energy attempting to appease others or trying to be perfect doesn't allow us to use our body for its true purpose. Rather than hustling just to stay ahead of everyone else, slow down and stop comparing. There is no need for a pursuit of perfection or trying to get ahead. And remember, it doesn't mean you're compromising dreams and goals. When we slow down and find rhythms of being, our dreams and goals may actually be served more thoroughly and rightly.

---

16  "Mindful Living," Slow Movement, https://www.slowmovement.com/slow_living.php (2007).

An important aspect to a healthy pace of life is our time of leisure. This can be spontaneous or intentional, and it is probably helpful when it is both. In regard to a spiritual way of living, we begin to recognize cultural tensions with our permission for leisure. More times than not, we will sense a twinge of guilt or shame when practicing leisure. Sister Joan Chittister says this, "Leisure, in other words, is an essential part of Benedictine spirituality. It is not laziness and it is not selfishness. It has to do with the depths and breadth, length and quality of life. In an American culture, however, leisure may also be one of the most difficult spiritual elements to achieve. We are trained to be doers and makers, not dreamers and seers."[17]

---

17   Sister Joan Chittister, *Wisdom Distilled from the Daily* (Harper Collins, 1991), 97.

*Chapter Eight*

# A Posture of Stillness

*If you keep the Sabbath, you start to see creation not as somewhere to get away from your ordinary life, but a place to frame an attentiveness to your life.*

**—Eugene H. Peterson**

There is an alarm sounding off these days, but many of us are ignoring it. I lament the fact that I allow myself to be extremely busy at times. With email, phone, texts, feeds dinging / ringing, the noise can drown out the "still small voice." This isn't something many of us have the ability to regulate. Life's demands are relentless at times. We are in desperate need of stillness.

In *The Shattered Lantern*, Ronald Rolheiser suggests that, "The way back to a lively faith is not a question of finding the right answers but living in a certain way. The existence of God, like the air we breathe, need not be proven. It is a question of developing good lungs to meet it correctly." These are words igniting my spirit in ways I know has God smiling. If we take the time to read, listen, and stop all the hustle and hurry, we will most certainly be surprised by what can occur in those moments, as well as how we can potentially be enabled to approach the remainder of the day.

I have found myself dreaming, reforming, and struggling to "keep it real" in regard to scheduling vs. stillness. Soul-care can easily give into the everyday demands we accrue. So many of us spend too much energy chasing trends and duty rather than allowing ourselves to be at peace with who we are wired and created to be. If we are honest with ourselves, the struggle of being genuine and authentic comes with a price that many of us find to be too high to pay. It begins in stillness. This stillness leads to becoming authentic. We can find ourselves vulnerable to criticism and judgment at this point. Some will most likely exploit authenticity to portray themselves in a specific light, holy, put together, and "normal." Anyone can be a sniper of negativity.

One of my most memorable moments of spiritual enlightenment, or of the presence of God, happened while in New Mexico. Over the years, I have heard many others mention their spiritually significant experiences from traveling to the Southwest, and New Mexico specifically.

I recall going for a run near Santa Fe one beautiful autumn day. The air was clear, crisp, and inviting. Back then, I would run between four to six miles on any given run. I believe I ran close to ten that day. The soundtrack to my effortless pace was of epic symphonic proportion. This is how I remember it, though it is possible it wasn't as legendary as my memory serves.

Upon returning to my hotel, I grabbed the book *New Seeds of Contemplation* by Thomas Merton, which an old friend had recommended a year or so prior. While reading against the backdrop of the Southwest mountains, I began to have a sense of God in one of the most comforting fashions I had ever been aware of. It was as though there was a palatable blanket of peace, belonging, and contentment. If I had ever truly made the time for being still and knowing that God was God, this was it (Psalm 46:10). I stopped reading and just sat in the holy stillness for several minutes. I have had many of these moments since.

Contemplation has been said to be the pursuit of meaning. A contemplative person believes that everything we do either advances or obstructs our search for meaning in life. Joan Chittister also says that those who find the will of God everywhere and feel the presence of God anywhere are the real contemplatives.[18] Not every moment needs to be memorable. The art of stillness is grounded in being present and mindful and doesn't have to be nostalgic or transcendent. The reality is that many of us may be conditioned to associate stillness with laziness and inactivity, and inactivity with failure. We are over-scheduled, overworked, and over-sensitized, and some of

18   Sister Joan Chittister, *Wisdom Distilled from the Daily*, 103.

us have come to believe that if, at any point, we aren't doing *something* that contributes to our income, we're not doing well.

This hinders us to "be still." In fact, we are *incredibly* opposed to idling. In a study done by the University of Virginia, over 700 people were asked to just sit in a room alone with their thoughts between six to fifteen minutes, alongside a shock button they could press if ever they wanted out. Sixty-seven percent of men and twenty-five percent of women *chose to shock themselves rather than sit quietly in stillness.*[19]

Stillness is psychologically imperative to our well-being, though. There are detrimental effects, the least of which I will touch on here. When over-performing becomes our identity, we begin to become something else entirely.

Our well-being depends on our abilities and willingness to be still. It's what humans are partially designed for. Tim Kreider writes in *The New York Times*[20], "Idleness is not just a vacation, an indulgence or a vice; it is as indispensable to the brain as vitamin D is to the body and, deprived of it, we suffer a mental affliction as disfiguring as rickets. The space and quiet that idleness provides is a necessary condition for standing back from life and seeing it whole, for making unexpected connections and waiting for the wild summer lightning strikes of inspiration—it is, paradoxically, necessary to getting any work done."

---

19  Ian Sample, "Shocking but true: students prefer jolt of pain to being made to sit and think," *The Guardian*, https://www.theguardian.com/science/2014/jul/03/electric-shock-preferable-to-thinking-says-study, (July 3, 2014).

20  Tim Kreider, "The 'Busy' Trap," *The New York Times*, https://opinionator.blogs.nytimes.com/2012/06/30/the-busy-trap, (June 30, 2012).

As one who currently leads liturgy and used to lead musical worship on Sundays, I try to observe and discern those in attendance. Most of us don't normally gravitate toward silence because we are afraid of what we will hear. Everyday noises drown out the centeredness and peace found in stillness. It is more difficult than ever to experience silence, much less rest in it for more than a few seconds. This is where the *Otherness* of God dwells. In the silent stillness, rest, we abide in the shadow of the Almighty.[21]

If all we focus on are the opinions, comments, trends, and the preferences of others, we'll never be truly centered beings. We arduously attempt to jump higher, run faster, and perform louder for the masses. Realistically, our private worship of the One will overflow into leading the response for many. If you are in a leadership role within a church, your personal devotion will inform your public devotion. Regardless of your personality, you cannot sustain the activity of a cheerleader for very long.

I have become very aware that many of us resist stillness in any variety. However, that doesn't lessen the importance or reality of our need for it. Early on, this popular prayer from Thomas Merton brought solace along my path of contemplation and stillness.

*My Lord God,*
*I have no idea where I am going.*
*I do not see the road ahead of me.*

---

21  Psalm 91:1 (ESV)

*I cannot know for certain where it will end, nor do I really know myself, and the fact that I think I am following your will does not mean that I am actually doing so.*

*But I believe that the desire to please you does in fact please you.*

*And I hope I have that desire in all that I am doing.*

*I hope that I will never do anything apart from that desire.*

*And I know that if I do this you will lead me by the right road, though I may know nothing about it.*

*Therefore, will I trust you always though I may seem to be lost in the shadow of death.*

*I will not fear, for you are ever with me, and you will never leave me to face my perils alone.*

*Chapter Nine*
# A Posture of Listening

In the continued development of counseling, priesthood, or Spiritual Direction, one seeks to improve listening techniques. Learning what it means to truly listen, to hear and comprehend is a gift. One isn't listening only to respond or reply. Listening to listen is a posture of empathy, civility, and discipleship. I would dare say that portions of society as well as the church could have avoided some of the fractures it has accumulated had humans become more astute to a posture of listening.

The art of listening moves us into a receptive mode of living. Being receptive requires a celebration and practice of Sabbath. Sabbath can become a season / time of receptivity.

*The Sabbath is a reminder of the two worlds—this world and the world to come; it is an example of both worlds.*
**—Abraham Joshua Heschel**

The benefits are more than helpful; they can be holy. In our modern observations, we have limited capacity to these ways of living, but that doesn't diminish the importance. Living in rhythms of attention, communion, slowing our pace, peace, and working for peace comes from a deep resting of Sabbath.

Our posture matters. Sacred rhythms embody opportunity to commune with our Creator and one another. Bad posture is unhealthy, physically and spirituality. Our intention and practice of listening implies that we are willing, interested, and available in the given moment. Over my years of ministry on church staffs, I have found it to be incredibly frustrating and disappointing to realize that pastors can be some of the worst of listeners. This isn't the case in all circles. I've found the more contemplative a clergy is, the better listener they can be.

*I think pastors are the worst listeners. We're so used to speaking, teaching, giving answers. We must learn to be quiet, quit being so verbal, learn to pay attention to what's going on, and listen.*
**—Eugene H. Peterson**

Today, while listening to the wind rattle some windows nearby, I had the sense that creation was saying something and that I should be paying attention. We never see the wind, only its effects. If faith is evidence of things unseen, maybe the wind is speaking a language we can only understand in the stillness.

Many times, when I have meetings outside of the office, I meet at one of my favorite local spots for coffee or a beverage. When I have some time in between my meetings, I tend to observe how obvious it is that we love to hear ourselves talk. Everyone is jumping over one another's words and phrases to express what each wants to say next. It's exhausting. Maybe that is what headphones are for from time to time.

This is a simple reminder that in hearing someone speak, we will hear what is said and what isn't said. Calming our agenda and opportunity to speak may help us actually comprehend what is being communicated. A posture of listening will particularly assist in our observations.

Some steps that may help a posture of listening:

- Take some deep breaths before beginning.
- Clear your mind of certain defaults in the conversation. Don't feel like you have to get a certain response or comment.
- Put mobile devices away or at least turn them over. I know we're all looking for the next Instagram photo op, but checking your phone is rude while conversing, regardless of our generation.
- Have a goal that is mindful of the other person. Make sure they leave knowing they have had an authentic conversation.

Cynicism is tiring, though sometimes it helps to give healthy motive and intention. It's helpful to speak less, listen more; fear less, hope more; do less, rest more; whine less, breathe more. Setting a posture of listening means we need to change our environment to be conducive to listening.

There is a stark contrast in responding vs. reacting. Reacting is typically more akin to what happens when something is thrown at you, a flinching of sorts. Responding lends more of a thoughtful, controlled action. In almost every situation, a patient, thoughtful, and consistent response is greater than a "wow and pow" moment of reaction.

A posture of reacting projects a reduced view of another person. Others require time, research, relational equity, and knowledge. This knowledge will eventually bring us understanding. May we not trespass on one another. It isn't your business to know every aspect of another unless they give us permission to be known at a deeper level.

Listening enables space for revelation over time. Frenzy only fuels the frantic. Many of us have a difficult time listening because we are afraid of what we may hear. This applies to personal private silence as well as the awkward pauses found at parties. When we become friends with silence, our listening will be enhanced, bringing about health that cannot be fabricated. The tension of faith and fear can be at play in almost every posture. Pay attention to the tension. There are layers to discover.

Here are three philosophical views relating to how we view reality:

1. **Idealism:** Reality that is mentally constructed, not what is "out there."
2. **Realism:** Reality is totally in the object "out there" regardless of the perception of it.
3. **Critical Realism:** The real truth is out there, but the human experience of it is a limited perception. The critical realism philosophy is compelling. Implying that if we can agree that there is indeed "truth" out there, then our task is the difficult work of honest dialogue, discussion, and debate.

This will result in a deep enrichment of the concept. Unexplored and un-debated, an idea of "truth" will remain small and unproven. The concept of enriching our life means that our faith, beliefs, and philosophies lend themselves to wonder, humility and, quite possibly, movement toward understanding and spiritual health.

*Chapter Ten*

# A Posture of Hope

*Prayer truly begins when we are finally silent.*
**—Soren Kierkegaard**

Hope is essential to life. Sometimes we forget about it until we realize our need for it. At times, the word hope itself seems empty and unattainable. But a posture of hope is one of prayer, meditation, and communion. Hope is mentioned anytime anyone aspires to encourage, rally, or inspire the masses. It resonates in our minds, hearts, and souls. It resonates because we are all in need of hope.

Winston Churchill said, "All the great things are simple, and many can be expressed in a single word: freedom, justice, honor, duty, mercy, hope." Hope teaches. Hope is active. Hope doesn't sleep. Hope stands up. What is hope? Without being exhaustive, hope can come from faith in the unseen; much like prayer, we have a heightened awareness of anticipation and centering of peace and hope.

I've often thought that prayer and meditation, or prayerful meditation if that helps, brings about a hopeful peace in that there is a not yet-ness to our being. Much of our discontent and frustration with prayer may be identified from our tendency to speak and only hear what we want to hear, if we hear anything at all. Our expectations should eventually deviate from a tight grip to a loose one in regard to communing with God in meditation and prayer. Dallas Willard said, "I'm practicing the discipline of not having to have the last word." This could be said of our posture of listening as well.

Fr. Richard Rohr explains: "Jesus taught and exemplified various forms of prayer. First, we notice the prayer of words in the Our Father where we are asked to "ask" and "knock" (Matthew 7:7) and then Jesus' prayer at the final supper. Over time, Believers have developed various forms of public and liturgical prayer, often centering around intercession, gratitude, and devotion. But Jesus also taught to pray beyond words: "praying in secret" (Matthew 6:5–6), "not babbling on as the Gentiles do" (Matthew 6:7), or his early morning, lonely prayer (Mark 1:35), because "your Father knows what you need even before you ask" (Matthew 6:8). These are all contemplative—communion with God's presence, resting and abiding with God more than seeking comprehension. Hope stirs from deep places.

Given Jesus' clear model and instruction, it seems strange that wordy prayer took over in the monastic Office, in the

Eucharistic liturgy, and in formulaic prayer like the Catholic rosary and Protestant memorizations. It's all the more important that these be balanced by prayer beyond words."[22]

*We must accept finite disappointment, but never lose infinite hope.*
**—Martin Luther King Jr.**

To find hope, to hold it close, to never let go of it. We need the means to practice the stillness and the language of prayer. The language of prayer may not be what you are accustomed to.

Prayer has historically been a source of hope for humanity. The connection with health and prayer has been studied for decades. Dr. Herbert Benson, a cardiovascular specialist at Harvard Medical School and a pioneer in the field of mind / body medicine, discovered what he calls "the relaxation response," which occurs during periods of prayer and meditation. His studies have found that the body's metabolism decreases, the heart rate slows, blood pressure goes down, and breathing becomes calmer.[23]

This state is correlated with slower brain waves and feelings of control, tranquil alertness, and peace of mind. This is significant because Benson estimates that over half of all doctor visits in the U.S. today are prompted by illnesses like depression,

---

22   Richard Rohr, *Things Hidden: Scripture as Spirituality* (St. Anthony Messenger Press, 2007), 121-124.
23   Richard Schiffman, "Why People Who Pray Are Healthier Than Those Who Don't," *HuffPost*, https://www.huffingtonpost.com/richard-schiffman/why-people-who-pray-are-heathier_b_1197313.html, (March 19, 2012).

high blood pressure, ulcers, and migraine headaches that are caused at least in part by elevated levels of stress and anxiety.

In the Scripture, we glean wisdom and insight. There is much to learn from the margins as well; those parts of the stories that aren't the main storyline. In most of the early text of Scripture where prayer is mentioned in original text, it actually means the combination of prayer *and* meditation. Praying words without pause, listening, and meditation is a reduced version of prayer. If we are more actively grasping for the words to voice our prayers instead of meditating on a passage or verse while being still and silent, we are missing the full meaning and purpose of prayer. Hope rings out in the stillness of prayer and meditation.

> *Hope, on one hand, is an absurdity too embarrassing to speak about, for it flies in the face of all those claims we have been told are facts. Hope is the refusal to accept the reading of reality which is the majority opinion; and one does that only at great political and existential risk. On the other hand, hope is subversive, for it limits the grandiose pretension of the present, daring to announce that the present to which we have all made commitments is now called into question.*
> —**Walter Brueggemann**, *The Prophetic Imagination*

The way of discernment begins with prayer. Praying means breaking through the veil of existence and allowing yourself to be led by the vision that has become genuine to you, whatever you call that vision. The one who prays to God pierces the darkness and senses the source of all being.[24] Before we know it, we become aware of our common life. A mantra of loving our neighbors as ourselves, caring for the least of these, and even being a voice for the voiceless. This insight not only informs us, it will profoundly compel our mindfulness of being the work of the people.

> *It begins in solitude and community, and the practice of what the Bible calls "distinguishing spirits" of truth and falsehood. Discernment is faithful living and listening to God's love and direction so that we can fulfill our individual calling and shared mission.*
> **—Henri Nouwen**

According to Evagrius of Pontus (345–399 AD), "Prayer is a laying aside of thoughts." A laying aside: not a savage conflict, not a furious repression, but a gentle yet persistent act of detachment. The Jesus Prayer, "Lord Jesus Christ, Son of God, have mercy on me, a sinner," is thus a prayer in words, but because the words are so simple, so few and unvarying, the prayer reaches out beyond words in the living silence of the Eternal.[25] This is contrary to what many of us have been taught. Many voices, such as Thomas Merton and Henri Nouwen, would say that prayer is more about listening than speaking.

---

24  Henri Nouwen, *With Open Hands* (Ave Maria Press), 114.
25  Kallistos Ware, The Power of the Name, Jesus Prayer in Orthodox Spirituality (Fairacres Publications), 17.

*Chapter Eleven*

# A Posture of Reconciliation

Reconciliation (noun)

1. an act of reconciling, as when former enemies agree to an amicable truce.
2. the state of being reconciled, as when someone becomes resigned to something not desired.
3. the process of making consistent or compatible.

Several years ago, I spent some time on a silent retreat where I was undone on levels I would have never imagined. There were many memorable moments from those days, though one specifically continues to stand out.

*Christian faith is… basically about love and being loved and reconciliation. These things are so important, they're foundational and they can transform individuals, families.*
—**Philip Yancey**

I was made mindful of a few people I hadn't realized I may have offended. I needed to right some wrongs. In a way, this is what confession does. In our liturgy, we confess to our wrongs toward God and one another. It is incredibly freeing and moving. So how do we translate this way of life to our every day?

My guess is that our arrogance and pride repel the light that comes with reconciliation. Where there is light, there can be no darkness. Darkness is where the toxins breed and grow. If you are in need of more peace in your life, pause and seek reconciliation where it is needed. Peace will eventually come.

We need the posture and work of reconciliation now more than ever, from our world's climate to our homes and families, our communities, our churches. The deep redemption found with reconciliation will change the way we live, and it will change those around us. One who finds peace with their inner self will not be able to help but affect those around them with a positive light.

Reconciliation begins with a posture of repentance. The forgiveness of Christ always precedes our repentance.

I've been a dreamer my whole life. My family would always talk about my imagination. I'll be honest, I still find myself pretending, imagining, and daydreaming. One of my favorite things to do these days is to watch my boys play together. They are quite creative and imaginative. My hope is that I will never hold them back but give them the wings to fly and pray that their Creator is their wind. One of the most freeing practices I have had is an abundance of opportunity to experience the practice of reconciliation. It frees the deepest and even most creative fragments of our being and propels the most audacious dreams ever dreamt.

As I grow older, I'm realizing that a person is not old until their regrets take the place of their dreams. The gravity of reconciliation and forgiveness construct a healthy path forward.

I've been extremely fortunate to have many people over the course of life who have given me wings to fly. Those wings were stages, platforms, partnerships, and opportunities. With all of the ridiculous decisions I've made over the years, I've learned from those mistakes. They have left scars. They have weighed me down and held me back. Without mentors and friends who have helped me pick myself up after I was knocked down, I now realize more than ever that I would not be able to dream to the extent I find myself dreaming.

For several years during my late twenties and early thirties, I was mentored by a dreamer. He taught me to risk, learn, grow, question, and dream. As a result of the creative experiences like recording, touring, and writing, I've learned to recreate community. Not only am I dreaming, I'm learning to be. Putting actions to your dreams will be what separates the "did it" from the "could've, should've." Everyone who supports an idea by joining in the effort is someone who is helping a dreamer take flight, but we should embody dreaming with our being.

By helping others dream, we join in the work of reconciliation. This intentional work brings about inspiration, and inspiration brings infectious hope. The need to "go and do likewise" begins to well up in each of us when we realize that we have been the recipient of forgiveness and grace.

> *To affirm and deepen our personal relationships with other human beings, it is not necessary to be continually presenting requests or using words; the better we come to know and love one another, the less need there is to express our mutual attitude verbally. It is the same in our personal relationship with God.*
>
> **—Kallistos Ware**

*Chapter Twelve*

# A Posture
# of Hospitality

A posture of hospitality is one who welcomes. It is an image of an open door and a seat saved at the table. Welcoming those alike as well as those who differ from ourselves.

I walked into a coffee shop last week where my gleeful mood soon changed to frustration and sadness. As I stood in the back of the line, I was witness to two acts of "barista abuse." The first, an older man in a suit ready to take on his day, evidently wanted a warm-up before getting into the daily flow at his office. He began to express his opinion on the barista's attitude and competence. The second offender, a younger lady, started off with a very short attitude over the ordering process. In my opinion, the lady didn't know how to order the drink that she was attempting to order... but she continued the venomous interaction. My guess is this barista didn't wake up that morning longing to have her competence questioned.

Needless to say, I was over the top with kindness once it was my turn. I did my best to apologize for the two before me. This bothered me all day. I don't know what was going on in the lives of the two customers in line ahead of me, but I was jarringly reminded of our fragility, and the importance of kindness. By the end of the very same day, I am certain I had failed in my own opportunities to be kind, loving, and even encouraging. In full disclosure, I am aware of how I operate when in a focused state. I tend to zone out and even respond with short / blunt comments (if I respond at all) so I can "get work done."

There is a time and place for blunt truth and critique. However, no one tends to receive truth when delivered without love or care. Some people enjoy being jerks or for being known as someone who doesn't pull any punches. Although being *nice* can be attractive, kindness has deeper meaning and intention. It is interesting to know that we will not find any Scripture where *nice* is technically found. However, we see that kindness is related to mercy, grace, and graciousness.

What if I said I knew one of the two persons who were the abusers of said barista? What if either of those abusers were you or me? What if we were the barista?

In a world where most people couldn't care less, what are we doing to be people who couldn't care more? Pride, insecurity, and apathy make life hard. Kindness can only help. If we were to wake up to a sense of the need to be more kind, more gentle, more loving, and more patient, we would see our lives turn from where they are to an improved place.

*Does the Lord take delight in thousands of rams, in ten thousand rivers of oil? Shall I present my firstborn for my rebellious acts, the fruit of my body for the sin of my soul? He has told you, O man, what is good; and what does the Lord require of you but to do justice, to love kindness, and to walk humbly with your God?26*

When taking this portion of text to heart, it can act as a filter to our attitude and awareness. True hospitality will come from a sensitive inclination of welcoming a stranger on their terms. Once we come to a centered place from within ourselves, we are more attentive and intentional with energy.

*If we should deal out justice only, in this world, who would escape? No, it is better to be generous, and in the end more profitable, for it gains gratitude for us, and love.*
**—Mark Twain**

As we develop a posture of hospitality, our sad divisions cease. Our "red" or "blue" bias lessens. Our judgment toward who is welcome at our tables begins to evolve into welcoming arms and adding more room to feast. Grace and kindness work well together. None can speak of grace without acting with kindness. Let's not wait for that magical elusive thing called relational equity in order to show kindness. It should be our driving force.

Acts of hospitality are acts of kindness, and kindness is the greatest wisdom. Compassion is a fruit of kindness.

---

26  Micah 6:7–8 (NASB)

*Compassion is the sometimes fatal capacity for feeling what it's like to live inside somebody else's skin. It is the knowledge that there can never really be any peace and joy for me until there is peace and joy finally for you too.*
**—Frederick Buechner**

In his book *The Meal Jesus Gave Us*, N.T. Wright offers a wonderful reflection: "Imagine life without parties. Imagine life without the thousand things we do, large and small, that give shape to who we are, that give extra meaning and value to people, to occasions, to the way we do things."[27]

A posture of hospitality offers meaningful room for *more*. More opportunity for conversation, more space to feel, be heard, and more space for listening.

For the years I toured, I had a favorite aspect of the travel. When booking repeating trips to the same cities, churches, and promoters, we began to form relationships and friendships with some of the most hospitable people across the country. These people were welcoming but not smothering. They always knew how to read the room or bus. When you needed extra space, they gave it graciously.

I recall being fairly ill on one trip to Indiana, Michigan, and Illinois. My bunk was my happy place. Well, that and homemade "cough medicine." This specific tour I was on the verge of losing my voice. Some friends from the area got wind of my illness and had care packages of all sorts of goodies to help ease my pain and frustration. Everything

---

27  N.T. Wright. *The Meal Jesus Gave Us* (Westminster John Knox Press, 2015), 5.

from tissue, throat lozenges, hot soup, tea, and even little shots of whiskey.

These small acts of kindness and hospitality got me through three states from the time I left home. One never knows the depth of meaning and care that can come from simple acts of kindness and hospitality.

# Section III
# WONDER

**Practice ten minutes of complete silence.**

*Religion points to that area of human experience where in one way or another man comes upon mystery as a summons to pilgrimage.*

**—Frederick Buechner**

*Chapter Thirteen*

# Paradox and the Unknown

*I always wondered why it took three days for significant things to happen in the Bible—Jonah spent three days in the belly of the whale, Jesus spent three days in the tomb, Paul spent three days blind in Damascus—and now I know. From earliest times people learned that was how long they had to wait in the dark before the sliver of the new moon appeared in the sky. For three days every month they practiced resurrection.*

—**Barbara Brown Taylor**, *Learning to Walk in the Dark*

We've all had questions without answers, been puzzled and frustrated at something that we just could not make sense out of. Maybe we've even encountered a paradoxical situation.

Almost everything in society hints of our longing for certainty and control. We tend to get a form of artificial satisfaction from the illusion of control, facts, and information we receive. Who likes to be left hanging on the edge of something unresolved or, worse, left with no means of resolve? I am seeing a trend in my circle of friends and colleagues. Some are coming to embrace mystery, un-resolve, even paradox. This should be encouraging in our pilgrimage toward spiritual health. Barbara Brown Taylor's quote above began a deep and lengthy process in me several years ago. There is a significant layer of mystery within the ancient text of Scripture.

What if we decided to not attempt to tame our childhood belief in mystery? As 1 Timothy 3:16 (MSG) says, "life is a great mystery, far exceeding our understanding." We might be able to get a form of comfort from knowledge and certainty, but inevitably there will come a longing for mystery; something larger than the confines of our cogitative capacity. That's when we step back and concede to awe for the Creator. If God is the beginning and the end (Alpha and Omega), we should have peace knowing that God knows all, and that we don't have to.

I wonder what would happen if we didn't live with such a rule of ego, pride, and control. Furthermore, what if we weren't crippled by narcissism? Oscar Wilde said that "Skepticism is the beginning of faith."[28] I am hopeful that groups of us are becoming more and more open to embracing mystery and even unimaginable paradoxes. Letting go can become a posture of

---

28   Oscar Wilde, *The Picture of Dorian Gray* (Courier Corporation).

worship and devotion. The commonly accepted opinions of faith are actually paradoxes in themselves... but when faith is the evidence of things unseen, this makes for some interesting tension. Embrace this tension. God is not the least bit threatened by our questions, concerns, or doubts.

> *In the Christian context, we do not mean by a "mystery" merely that which is baffling and mysterious, an enigma or insoluble problem. A mystery is, on the contrary, something that is revealed for our understanding, but which we never understand exhaustively because it leads into the depth or the darkness of God. The eyes are closed—but they are also opened.*
> **—Kallistos Ware**

Everyone has questions without adequate answers, and we can become puzzled and frustrated at something that we just can't make sense out of. God, faith, death... life.

Almost everything in society is fact / control-oriented. We tend to get a form of temporary satisfaction from the control, facts, and information we receive. Who likes to be left hanging on the edge of something unresolved? Honestly, I want resolve and control. I don't know many people who don't. I even see it in worship gatherings I'm a part of. People are afraid of letting go of what they feel they have control of—emotions, expression, response, and yeah... worship.

There was a time not so long ago that I enjoyed life's mysteries. I would embrace things that I didn't fully comprehend. The world has tried to poison us to believe that we will find the peace and satisfaction we need in certainty, simplistic logic, and control. In doing so, this takes the magic out of faith. *Faith isn't faith until it's all you're holding on to.*

A life that follows Jesus will be repeatedly tempted to fall prey to the comprehension game if we don't surrender ourselves to the mysterious awe of God that is being beaten out of us by life itself.

*Wonder rather than doubt is the root of all knowledge.*
**—Abraham Joshua Heschel**

We might be able to get a form of comfort from knowledge and control, but there will come a longing for supernatural mystery. That's when I want to step back and let awe for the Creator overwhelm me. If God is the beginning and the end, we should have peace knowing that God knows all, and we don't have to. That probably won't stop us from trying to know it all though. I guess we can hope and trust that through walking out our faith in the real world, God will meet us where we are and guide us with His Spirit to mystery, reality, logic, and truth.

Astonishment seems to be a thing of the past. We're living in a time of excess, where there is too much noise, information, and opinion. No one is listening, and we've somehow allowed our wonder to be eroded from our devotion.

*Outdoors we are confronted everywhere with wonders; we see that the miraculous is not extraordinary but the common mode of existence.*
**—Wendell Berry**

"Time has become the incarnation of scarcity. The Gregorian calendar is what we live by; it was invented for Easter and became useful for commerce. But the reality is that it was made up. Time zones were made to assist the British Navy. There is always time, no matter how busy we become. In consumer society, time is a scarcity. The biggest shift in consciousness is away from thinking, 'I don't have time.' So much of our traveling is still in the time-is-running-out world. Busyness, or lack of time, is the common argument against Democracy."[29]

Faith is the assurance of things hoped for, the conviction (or evidence) of things not seen.[30] If "wonder is the basis of worship," as Thomas Carlyle said, maybe we should allow ourselves to be astonished once again. This could possibly be the conviction and evidence of things unseen due to the faith we slowly begin to embody.

Leaning into the activity of God is to allow for great mystery and curious joy. This will continually lead us into the gravity of holiness. Not in the sense that we may think of holiness, but it is nonetheless. As image bearers of our Maker, we have curiosity and a need to acknowledge mystery coded into our DNA. It compels our imagination to search for, unearth, and create beauty. Not all beauty is bright, shiny, or clean. Something flawed, broken, and dark can be deeply beautiful. Curiosity for the mysterious Otherness can be found in the undercurrent of our being.

---

29  Block, Brueggemann, and McKnight, An Other Kingdom: Departing the Consumer Culture.
30  Hebrews 11:1 (ESV)

I am learning to hold obtuseness in higher regard rather than religious confidence. Sisters and brothers along The Way, as we resonate with similar outlooks along the path, be encouraged. May our tables leave a place set for the grandeur and wonder of things unseen.

*We go out from the known to the unknown, we advance from light into darkness. We do not simply proceed from the darkness of ignorance into the light of knowledge, but we go forward from the light of partial knowledge into a greater knowledge which is so much more profound that it can only be described as the "darkness of unknowing."*
**—Kallistos Ware**

*Chapter Fourteen*

# Estrangement

I grew up with some interesting and challenging circumstances. Like so many others, I grew up without my biological father in the daily picture. My mother and father were divorced around the time I was a year old. I grew up with a stepfather and had a different last name from anyone else in my home. For years, I didn't know what to think about my biological father. There was a feeling of detachment that an eight-year-old shouldn't have to process. There were all types of complicated layers to my upbringing. As I grew up and became more aware, I found out that I had a half-brother whom I had never met. I also had a stepsister and stepbrother who didn't live in our home but came to visit from time to time.

I found it odd when my stepbrother stopped visiting, only to learn that when he came out as being gay, my stepfather essentially disowned him. My stepbrother went on to distance himself from his father to the point of legally changing his name. This is interesting to think in the light of some biblical stories. God changing people's names to leave who they were only gives them a new future. The wounds my stepbrother acquired were too bloody and too much. He started a new life without his father in it.

Estrangement is one of the most misunderstood words of our days and yet can be traced back to activity in the Scripture. Throughout history, humans have had an estranged relationship with their Maker. Some of us make efforts to move as far away from God as we can and even change our names—as if God wouldn't be able to find us. Those who can identify as someone who is "de-churched" may be able to resonate with the idea of letting go of a painful past yet attempt to continue some level of devotion to their faith. We may be surprised to find God will always know, care, and love us regardless of where we go and what we do. Shame isn't a weapon of God's.

Estrangement is to turn away in feeling or affection; make unfriendly or hostile; alienate the affections of. This doesn't cause you to lose your sense of belonging or your namesake. When we begin to resolve and restore relationships, we are rejoined with our family. Much like the Eucharist, we are put back together (re-membered) as we remember Christ's death, resurrection, and life. This God is a mystery to be explored and revered, not contained and controlled. The more we can get our head and hearts around this, the healthier we will begin to be over time.

We are living in the tension of the already and the not yet. In a macro picture, events and history have happened and are happening—and there are things that have not yet come to pass. Don't pretend you didn't re-read that in the voice of Galadriel from *The Lord of the Rings*.

There are means to broaden our worldview and expand our hearts and minds. The process of self-discovery is always the best medium of retention. Once you experience something for yourself, a lecture or sermon simply won't measure up. Once our hearts and minds broaden, we are conditioned for more and more wonder to the point of awe. This can actually become a new normal for us eventually.

If we were all honest, we would probably agree that when we were growing up, we all wanted to be considered "normal." Most of us wanted to blend in, not stand out. Until we become a bit more comfortable in our own skin, we will probably be hesitant of standing out in a crowd. Not many want to set out into a life of estrangement. Normalcy seems a bit more attractive, but there are even nuanced tensions in the "normal."

*Nobody realizes that some people expend tremendous energy merely to be normal.*
**—Albert Camus**

At one point in life just a few years ago, I resolved to honestly believe that I was well adjusted, balanced, and centered on who I was made to be. I felt I had no estrangement or enemies. One day I woke up and realized that I did indeed have some estranged relationships and I actually had "enemies." This was a flaw in the framework of my expectations. At that moment, I recognized that I will never be fully "comfortable" in my own skin, and that may be a positive reality check. I'm also realizing that I'll never be completely "normal," nor will you, and *that* is a good thing. The long pilgrimage of understanding expectations begins with managing them. Management isn't the same as controlling.

I spent my twenties on the road touring. One of my favorite things about touring was all of the reading I was able to do in my coffin-like bunk. I read everything from philosophy, history, and theology books from the likes of C.S. Lewis, Madeleine L'Engle, Thomas Merton, and countless others. This began the journey toward self-awareness that, the more I read, the less I seemed to know. The more self-discovery, the less sure I was of what I have always been so sure about. That may sound like deconstruction. And I just believe it may have been, before it was "a thing."

Once I stumbled upon the contemplative life, I felt encouraged to pursue a deep dive of what it meant to truly be. It was almost like I finally received permission from my Creator to begin to understand who I had been created to be. In my brief experience in faith, church, and the tempting to be a disciple of Jesus, I was never given permission to believe anything other than what I was told to believe. But the more I spent time in stillness and silence, and slowed my speaking of prayers, is when

I began to hear God in ways beyond words. My communion began to deepen little by little.

I began to see God in all things and slowly began to see all things in God. So, the process of self-awareness began in the stillness and continues the deepening in the stillness. This isn't retreating or escapism but, instead, is a way of engaging and navigating life on a day-to-day basis. In this still space, we find a pace that enables our awareness of God, our awareness of others, and where our place is. Some of the most important finds of my first forty-something years:

1. Cultivate space for margin.
2. Build it into your schedule or allow it to build your schedule if you are fortunate enough.
3. Simplify, lessen the stress you put on yourself by living at an unsustainable pace, so true communion can reoccur.

We would do well to grasp the concept of being estranged more than separated. There is a layer of grace here in the difference of the two.

*Chapter Fifteen*
# Mysteriousness

Throughout history, light has been associated with sacredness. The English definition for Sacred:

1. secured against violation, infringement, etc., as by reverence or sense of right.
2. properly immune from violence, interference, etc., as a person or office.

The Greek word *hágios* means different (unlike), other ("otherness"), holy; "likeness of nature with the Lord," "different from the world."

During my early days of touring, I was fortunate enough to spend a few days in Alaska. This was a fascinating trip. On one of our days off, a bandmate and I were taken up in a single-engine propeller plane with four seats. We may have been in the air for over an hour or so before we flew over a massive glacier. The pilots were explaining the scale of what we were seeing all while trying to reassure us of our safety as the crosswinds tossed us about.

As we began our descent, we were told that we would be eating dinner at the top of the mountain we just flew over. On the gondola ride to the top with our new friends, they continued their riveting explanation of Alaskan culture. After finishing dinner, they said, "We will go to the other side of the range so we can see the aurora borealis (northern lights)."

I must say, the lights were brilliant. Mystical, even. You can view all the photos you want on Google, but there is no substitute for live viewing. Though it was minus 30 degrees Fahrenheit and I couldn't feel my face for the next fifteen hours, it was breathtaking (pun intended). You truly couldn't breathe out there. Even so, I will never forget that experience.

The combination of wonder and scale that I sensed above and atop the Alaskan glaciers and mountains cannot be fully articulated. This very well may be a proper example of what wonder actually feels like. There are no words, and when attempting to find them, they would not suffice. I will only say, before that day in Alaska, I had never been aware of such astonishment and mysteriousness.

*We will always reflect the nature of the world we are most aware of.*
**—Bill Johnson**

Do you remember the phrase "You are what you eat"? That phrase used to irritate me. I was always a pizza. But there's truth to the fact that what we take in, read, watch, and listen to all affect us in some way. It's inescapable. Whatever we consume, we become—we all know this. And whatever is inside of us (good or bad) eventually comes out.

So, it makes sense that if we see light in each other's lives, if something bright and beautiful is coming out, then there is probably a source for that light buried deep inside.

Our eyes have an interesting relationship with light. Whatever we "see" is actually what is being reflected back to us. Similarly, whatever people see of us is simply what the light is revealing. The light shines in the darkness, and it reveals what would rather remain hidden. "A city set on a hill cannot be hidden…"[31]

Our awareness of the sources of light can be underestimated at times. We won't be able to heal what is broken if we are oblivious to the brokenness. We need the light to shine. Some light is harsh—it pierces through the shadows and can blind us. Other light is soft and subtle—our eyes gradually get used to it and we begin to see things clearly. But all light reveals.

We need more saturation of light in our lives; we need more awareness of what we do not yet know. There is an abundant need for more margin, stillness, and discipline as we learn to listen and train our eyes to see what the light is revealing. Just as our eyes need time to adjust as we go into the darkness, our eyes also require time to adjust to the light once we come out of the dark.

---

31  Matthew 5:14 (ESV)

There was a time not so long ago that I enjoyed life's mysteries. I would embrace things that I didn't fully comprehend. The world has tried to poison me (and you) to believe that we will find the peace and satisfaction we need in facts, logic, and control. In doing so we are diminishing the wonder out of faith. What if we decided that we weren't going to let society tame our childhood belief in mystery the way St. Paul speaks of in 1 Timothy 3:16? The Message translation says, "This…life is a great mystery, far exceeding our understanding." A life that follows Jesus will fall prey to the comprehension game if we don't surrender ourselves to the mysterious awe of God.

*Chapter Sixteen*

# Thin Places

In the Celtic tradition, "thin places" are where the veil that separates heaven and earth is nearly transparent. It is a place where we experience a deep sense of God's presence in our everyday world. A thin place is where, for a moment, the spiritual world and the natural world intersect. There are moments when we do feel the divine breaking through into the dimension of our world. We feel unified and connected with God. It is not an intellectual knowing, it is felt in the spirit. It can be a sudden momentary awareness or profound unexplainable experience. I encourage you to have eyes to see and ears to hear the thin places. The phenomenon of a place where the physical and natural everyday world merges into a thin line is well-rooted in biblical history, but it was the Celts who gave the descriptive phrase "thin place" to it.

> *"Thin places," the Celts call this space,*
> *Both seen and unseen,*
> *Where the door between the world*
> *And the next is cracked open for a moment*
> *And the light is not all on the other side.*
> *God-shaped space. Holy.*
> **—Sharlande Sledge**

The Celts were a culture of people who arrived in Ireland after 500 BC. The idea of thin places or doorways to the Otherworld were solidly a part of the Irish culture long before the Celts came. Newgrange passage tomb is 5,200 years old and has entrance stones with large spirals carved into the surface, common symbols for the pre-Christian Irish—and linked to their concept of thin places.[32]

Life is best understood backward but must be experienced forward, to paraphrase Soren Kierkegaard. After decades of wandering, only now does a pattern emerge. I'm drawn to places that beguile and inspire, sedate and stir, places where, for a few blissful moments, I loosen my death grip on life and can breathe again. It turns out these destinations have a name: thin places. It is, admittedly, an odd term.

One could be forgiven for thinking that thin places describe skinny nations (like Chile) or perhaps cities populated by thin

---

32  "Richard Rohr—The Celts Didn't Invent Thin Places," http://www.
thinplace.net/2011/03/richard-rohr-celts-didnt-invent-thin.html.

people (like Los Angeles). No, thin places are much deeper than that. They are locales where the distance between heaven and earth seems to collapse and we're left able to catch glimpses of the divine or the transcendent or, as I like to think of it, the infinite whatever. Travel to thin places does not necessarily lead to anything as grandiose as a "spiritual edge of things." The thin places concept was a part of the pre-Christian or pagan charism and these beliefs or sensitivities existed prior to the Celts. The concept is rejected by many of the present-day Christian communities, often being linked to "new age" movements.

Fr. Richard Rohr wrote, "To take your position on the spiritual edge of things is to learn how to move safely in and out, back and forth, across and return. It is a prophetic position…"[33] He uses this phrase not to relate that the *place* where you physically stand (on the edge) puts you in a prophetic position. He's writing about something ephemeral or of the consciousness or mind. The physical place doesn't appear to have any significance in his definition; however, we can see that when our awareness of God is heightened, thin places will potentially become thin moments regardless of the place.

These pre-Christian Irish people believed the thin place itself had mystical or spiritual power. One didn't create a thin place simply by moving into a state of contemplation or spiritual trance. The site itself was thin and that made spiritual contemplation more compelling.

---

33   Richard Rohr, "Life on the Edge: Understanding the Prophetic Position," *HuffPost*, https://www.huffingtonpost.com/fr-richard-rohr/on-the-edge-of-the-inside_b_829253.html, (May 25, 2011).

I hear many people in search of a "breakthrough," whatever that means. I am coming to find this need for revelation or "breakthrough" comes from being disoriented. With life, we lose our bearings and find new ones, and sometimes we don't. Either way, we are jolted out of an old way of seeing the world, and therein lies the transformative magic of travel. It's not clear who first coined the term "thin places," but they almost certainly spoke with an Irish brogue. The ancient pagan Celts, and later, Christians, used the term to describe mesmerizing places like the wind-swept isle of Iona (now part of Scotland).

Heaven and earth, the Celtic saying goes, are only three feet apart, but in thin places that distance is even shorter. So, what exactly makes a place thin? It's easier to say what a thin place is not. A thin place is not necessarily a tranquil place, or a fun one, or even a beautiful one, though it may be all of those things too. Thin places bring us an awareness of something "Otherly." Sometimes they give us a sense of scale. Something as vast as a mountain range or mountain peak, or possibly something ancient. A blissful moment of relaxation, where transcendence is reminiscent of heaven meeting earth, can give us a centering that brings peace and perspective. Perspective itself can be a thin place. Thin places have a tendency to transform us—or, more accurately, reveal us. In thin places, we become our true selves.

> *But as for me, the nearness of God is my good; I have made the Lord God my refuge, that I may tell of all Your works.*[34]

---

34   Psalm 73:21–28 (NASB)

Thin places are often sacred ones. Thin places come in different ways and some can be subtle. I call them "Garden of Eden moments" because they remind me of the way things must have been in the Garden of Eden when the earth was perfect and at peace. I think we have all experienced them, kind of a time of unified joy. The bounty and beauty of nature can bring such joy: a sunrise or sunset, the coming of spring, or a deep winter snow.

Meditation is a vital tool for strengthening our self in the Lord. When our focus changes, our thoughts follow—and then our feelings. When we go to a "sanctuary" and meditate and ponder, *I AM* encourages us and teaches us. God deposits His Word and self into our heart and our mind. And sometimes, sometimes we find ourselves in a thin place. God is good, and God is love.

# Section IV

# RECONSTRUCTION

**Practice fifteen minutes of complete silence.**

*O my merciful Redeemer, Friend, Brother,*
*May I see you more clearly, love thee more dearly, and*
*follow thee more nearly.*
　　　　—Invocation of St. Richard of Chichester

*Chapter Seventeen*

# Post-Church

The Judeo-Christian tradition was not meant to be a top-down experience, but an organic meeting between an Inner Knower (Holy Spirit) accessed by prayer and being, and the ancient text and tradition (all the ancestors). This is a calm and healing way to acknowledge that we are not the first to be on this path, nor will we be the last.[35]

Many of us have been in the process of deconstruction, whether we knew it at the time or not. A long and grueling experience probably led us into the process. Traumatic or even abusiveness from church leadership has played no evangelical / mainline favorites throughout history. It is unfortunate to think that the modern church felt as though crafting an environment

---

35    Richard Rohr, *Things Hidden: Scripture as Spirituality*, 119-121.

that feels more like the theatre or arena would be the answer to deformation, ill-formation, and spiritual malnutrition when followers of Christ, as well as the curious, were simply in need of peace and forgiveness, not more dogma and doctrine.

We cannot settle the confusions of our time by pretending to have absolute answers. We must not give up seeking out truth, observing our reality from all angles. Richard Rohr says, "We settle human confusion not by falsely pretending to settle all the dust, but by teaching people an *honest and humble process for learning and listening*, which we call contemplation. Then people come to wisdom in a calm and compassionate way. There will not be the knee jerk overreactions that we have in so many on both Left and Right today."[36]

In general, the Episcopal Church was birthed for those who couldn't technically remain a part of the Church of England. Episcopal bishops continued the beauty and comfort of what they knew and loved and gave more and more opportunity for new expressions to emerge and expand with new versions of ecclesial practices. New frontier settlers found themselves wary of Rome and Canterbury; stretched thin by geographical distance and culture, many used these new times as a way of continuing reformation. The American church (as well as others) bears the weighty shame of sanctioning slavery and genocide. And as ridiculous as it can be, it seems that Christians never behave more anti-Christ-like toward the world than when they believe they are protecting God or their version of God.

---

36 Richard Rohr, "Listening and Learning," Center for Contemplation and Action, https://cac.org/listening-and-learning-2018-10-04, (October 4, 2018).

The number of white evangelical Protestants fell from about 23 percent of the US population in 2006 to 17 percent in 2016, and only 11 percent are under thirty, according to a survey of more than 100,000 Americans.[37] This is one of many findings. However, the truth is there are declines almost straight across the board. Mainline Protestants have been on the decline for decades. It's not hopeless, it is simply a cycle of our reality.

Yet the Church, though battered and scared, has endured much. This surely reaches beyond institutional endurance. Centuries of pride, anger, envy, gluttony, and lust—coverups, sexual misconduct, and abuse—just to name a few. Some large church systems seem to even thrive in almost every economic or social climate. Sometimes sanctuaries are just that; regardless of their affiliation—Evangelical, Catholic, Anglican, or Lutheran—they can sometimes be a final effort for people who have other cultural connections like sports, clubs, and the like. The Church should attempt to preserve language that elevates the mind out of the cluttered and noisy minutiae of society.

*With so much effort being poured into church growth, so much press being given to the benefits of faith, and so much flexing of religious muscle in the public square, the poor in spirit have no one but Jesus to call them blessed anymore.*

—**Barbara Brown Taylor**, *Leaving Church: A Memoir of Faith*

---

37  "America's Changing Religious Landscape," *Pew Research Center*, http://www.pewforum.org/2015/05/12/americas-changing-religious-landscape, (May 12, 2015).

Grace seems to be here one day and gone the next, nowhere to be found due to circumstances or convenience. There is always more to do and more to give as well. Pace and temperance aren't traditional strong suits. Many modern theologians have asked whether or not western evangelicals are only capable of thinking for an abbreviated portion of time and only to a more shallow depth with the sole objective to be "right." This is generally speaking, of course. I know some wonderfully gracious and brilliant evangelicals.

There are numerous reasons people choose to not to be a part of a church. Here are just a few that may resonate with you: Some churches are too exclusive. They have a house style. Long-time parishioners know all the moves, liturgical and social. They refer to their favorite person of the Trinity in a socially correct way. There appears to be a dress code, casual, trendy, or dressed up.

Some churches oversimplify the complexities of life and dismiss reality. Over the centuries, the Church began attempting to manage people's morality. This can be translated from a place of good motive, but it unfortunately became unmanageable and poisonous. Moving into modern times, the Church started trying to answer questions no one was asking. Maybe the question shouldn't be "If I die, will I go to heaven?" Instead, it should be "But while I am alive, will I bring heaven to earth?"

Sermons tend to oversimplify the gospel message but only the parts that pertain to a rather insular range of concerns, with a heavy emphasis on comfort rather than challenge. Some would rather that people leave church being affirmed of the way they already live, though it would seem that most leave feeling thirsty, restless, and confused, or even disoriented.

Replicating popular culture is a farce. We need to enable a space to commune with God, rather than producing a "show." Sometimes, but not always, this involves screens, haze, and lots of performing musicians. Sometimes, it involves awkwardly singing along to catchy love songs. Most of the time it is brand-heavy. The church logo is everywhere. Some notion of a common denominator appears to determine style of worship at the expense of substance and reverence as though relevance and reverence cannot co-exist.

Some churches are simply too partisan. The political climate today has become combustible to say the least. When churches openly support candidates and single-issue voting, rather than nuanced reflection on doctrine, they become incredibly biased and too shaded. Over the course of time, these places will recede or even die after their base changes or eventually moves on. The Gospel transcends cultural and political belief systems. The Church and leaders are obviously entitled to their own opinions and leanings, but we shouldn't be at war over these opinions. When Christ isn't the center, something or someone else is.

At some point, for many people, faith and practice were important or even life-giving, but it lost its shine over time. Traditionally, this involves a level of visible hurt, frustration, or traumatizing experience, but not always. Sometimes, people are just tired of the bull$#!%. As tempting as it is, we shouldn't throw baby Jesus out with the bath water.

Over the years I would say that we have never been worse human beings than when we think we are protecting God or something godly.[38] This belief echoes throughout history. No wonder some allow their frustrations with other Believers to taint their awe of Jesus. Over time, we may see that a reentry into the Church is more of a realization that we were never cut off from her to begin with.

The reasons people choose not to belong to a church are unfortunate and can be discouraging. You and I both know this list could go on for numerous chapters. But here's some encouragement: If we were to make a list of reasons to be a part of a church more interesting, then I'd be glad to share with the cynical, the indifferent, and the uninformed. It's not an indiscriminate invitation to hasten out next Sunday seeking the nearest steeple, but a challenge to find, even if it takes some church-hopping, those places where the Spirit is working quiet wonders among ordinary people. The reluctant and skeptical have their reasons to be. I would remind us that the pilgrimage of the Christian life is about coming to the end of ourselves and that there is no reconstruction without movement.

*Theology became increasingly specialized and systematized. Our "God view" came to resemble our worldview. In many places, it is still possible to hear God described as a being who behaves almost as predictably as Newton's universe. Pull this lever and a reward will drop down. Do not touch that red button, however, or all hell will break loose. In this clockwise universe, the spiritual quest is reduced to*

---

38  Barbara Brown Taylor, *Leaving Church: A Memoir of Faith*, (HarperOne, 2012).

*learning the rules in order to minimize personal loss (avoid hell) and maximize personal gain (achieve salvation).*
—**Barbara Brown Taylor**, *The Luminous Web*

A healthy church environment will help you come to the end of yourself. Christ-centric teaching invites us into a narrative that is much bigger than our own single story. The vast meaning of being a part of the "one, holy, catholic, and apostolic Church" begins to emerge over time. Healthy churches are open to conversations of depth and pain as well as the portions of life we attempt to leave in the dark due to the social or culture climate of "what would people think" types of tensions. Healthy environments are grateful places. Church isn't about attendance; it's about communion. Grateful people will be compelled to be in attendance because of the energy that develops.

Healthy places empower the Body to be the liturgy (work of the people). When you experience this, our issues and frustrations eventually become defused and decompressed. Self-awareness turns to self-motivated discipleship. Standing, kneeling, listening, and helping become more of the church's posture and tendencies instead of judgment, hypocrisy, ignorance, and shallowness. Empathy and compassion breed forgiveness, joy, and fullness of life. Injustices can no longer hide in the darkness and shadow, because the Light becomes too great.

Racial reconciliation and advocacy become a part of the fabric of our hopes, beliefs, and rhythms. On the way, we begin to allow truth to break through our privilege and prejudices.

We find ourselves immersed in healthy sacred spaces where the effects of worshiping from a place of devotion changes the way we see community. Spiritual health opens us up to seeing the world through the eyes of the Gospel instead of manmade portals of bias and contempt.

The Greek word *schizomeno*, meaning "ripped open," occurs two times in the Gospels. Once, when the temple veil is torn the day of Christ's crucifixion. The second when "heaven opened" at Christ's baptism. This wasn't simply an "opening." They were ripped open. God broke through into history with the narrative of hope, redemption, and life. A dramatic moment to say the least, and it would be easy to overlook without the Greek translation to assist our vantage in English.

Even though there is a long laundry list of offenders who may have influenced our view of the Church, not everyone is guilty. The Church certainly needs to return to a Sacred Place. There are very few places left for people to gather, sing, and truly commune together. It would serve us well to realize that neuroscientists have said that singing together tends to promote integration of multiple brain functions and alleviates levels of depression, all while promoting mental wellness. There are mysterious occurrences in the midst of people singing, praying, and expressing lament, need, joy, and celebration. Some of us are more wired than others for excited levels of engagement in these kinds of environments. Introverts, for example, are usually made to feel like something is wrong with them when we cannot connect with a "Christian pep rally." Sacredness transcends spectacle.

Hearing the Ancient Texts read aloud provides us with a grounding alignment with others who are a part of the same narrative. It is our story, all of us. And the Eucharist—the Lord's Supper, Holy Communion—is the place of being re-membered (put back together) in our remembering. When we walk forward or kneel for Communion, we experience the real presence of Christ. We would do well to recall that this is a gift that we receive, not simply a piece of food that we take. Think of it as intentional posture of receiving. A taking posture is quite another thing entirely.

Not all churches are alike. Frankly, not all churches are healthy. The troubles that afflict unhealthy churches are nothing new: they are disheveled or diseased or fatigued or torn by infighting. But even those churches contain within themselves the seeds of renewal. They aren't simply dying institutions, irrelevant and poorly run; they are cell and tissue of the body of Christ.[39] Within them people we may not enjoy but must engage with are, in very fact, brothers and sisters who belong to us and to whom we belong by a tie stronger than blood. All of us who labor and are heavy-laden come to receive "the gifts of God for the people of God" and find that God's people are also our people.

Now more than ever in our modern time have more people affiliated themselves as a "None," meaning they don't really have a faith. It's not that they are atheist, or even agnostic. A theist is someone who has a faith and an atheist is someone having no faith; both can sometimes find common ground. I would argue

---

39 Marilyn McEntyre, "Choosing Church," *Comment*, https://www.cardus.ca/comment/article/choosing-church, (September 1, 2017).

more times than not that when we don't lead with our faith but instead lead with our humanity, a common good is a common goal. However, many Christians throughout the course of history have had problems being human and as it's been said, maybe they're too heavenly minded to be any earthly good; they view their faith as an evacuation plan for when everything here burns. But many of us are finding that faith is more about finding a way to live in the light of the life of Christ, loving our neighbor as ourselves, treating others as we would like to be treated, leaving the world better than we found it. As N.T. Wright likes to say, it's more about the colonization of earth with the kingdom of heaven.

*Chapter Eighteen*

# Not Alone

*Christian Spirituality is never something you do alone.*
**—Ronald Rolheiser**

Some days I recall and pray a portion of response from my ordination and pursuit of Holy Orders: "with God's help," a simple but meaningful posturing upon receiving the weight of minister. In this, we can see that we are never really meant to be separated from others, especially our Creator. "With God's help" implies that alone, we can't nor shouldn't, but with God, we can and should.

We were not meant to live alone, in isolation. Believers were never meant to exclusively interpret Scripture on their own. For it is in community that we learn, grow, navigate, and form.

Forming our worldview in isolation will inevitably leave us with a bland and possibly harsh posture toward those we differ from. "We" will always be the way forward, not "I."

Let's not mistake intentional personal solitude as a negative. This premeditated space is essential to our well-being and spiritual health. It is worth noting the significance of the wilderness throughout the narrative of Scripture. David, Moses, and Christ all had a wilderness. God's activity and presence can and will be anywhere, especially where you may least expect it.

We talk a lot about relationships and community in church, probably to the point of it being more noise than meaning. And still, I'm not so great at authentic community. As an introvert, I find that I allow a very small group of people into my "inner circle." While having many in my "friendship circle" and even more in the "outer circle," finding true relationships is actually hard work, draining even.

We can be very conditional and even political, but true friendship comes with no conditions and most certainly shouldn't be a strategic political move. True community and friendship shouldn't be competitive... Nor should our communities of faith be.

Do we allow ourselves to be as real as possible with others, especially our friends? Consistently, I doubt it. I know we can't go "all in" with everyone we meet or work with, but there should be a level of security, loyalty, and trust with those who know us best.

*A friend is one who walks in when others walk out.*
**—Walter Winchell**

I have not always been a true friend. To those, I am sorry. Life is indeed too short to allow lesser moments to bind away the fullness of life that we can all find in real relationships. I have been blessed with a great group of friends over the years. My hope is that I can attempt to be a friend in return to those who call me friend. Here is a reminder to how we should process... 1 Corinthians 13 (MSG) says,

> Love never gives up.
> Love cares more for others than for self.
> Love doesn't want what it doesn't have.
> Love doesn't strut,
> Doesn't have a swelled head,
> Doesn't force itself on others,
> Isn't always "me first,"
> Doesn't fly off the handle,
> Doesn't keep score of the sins of others,
> Doesn't revel when others grovel,
> Takes pleasure in the flowering of truth,
> Puts up with anything,
> Trusts God always,
> Always looks for the best,
> Never looks back,
> But keeps going to the end.

What would you say is one of the biggest reasons we resist community and real friendships?

Every few years I find myself in a season of redefining, redirecting, and recalibrating life. Maybe it's just the beginning of a new year, I don't know. With a new year comes a bit of nostalgia with a side of sentimentalism.

The definition of "friend." It is an overused and diluted word, and even sometimes a forgotten one. We are using it in a social media stream every day. I've been on Facebook since it was a college platform. It was terrible back then; however, less noisy. Before I transferred my profile page to a music page, I began to go thru some of my "friends" on Facebook, only to find that I can't possibly have *that* many friends. True. I accept almost anyone (anyone wearing clothing in their profile pic). I don't use it as my primary medium of connection to everyday friends. I do enjoy casually keeping up with people from school, sports, road life, etc.

Friend:

noun

1. a person attached to another by feelings of affection or personal regard.
2. a person who gives assistance; patron; supporter.
3. a person who is on good terms with another; a person who is not hostile.

I have always had many instances where I would say "yeah, I'm friends with them," but I'm not, if I were really honest. Just because we know someone doesn't mean we're friends by the definition of the word. And, that's okay. Knowing who we are, what drains us, what fills us, and what inspires us will alter who we are and how we live. We need to invest our time, emotions, and life in others who bring us life. That will also give us the strength to be the encouragers we need to be with others who may be a little more "trying" or draining.

Take this in. "Outgrowing" relationships isn't a bad thing, nor does it negate what once was. Sometimes we can honor each other by moving on.

The Greek word for community is *koinonia*, which means communion, joint participation, fellowship and the unity that should exist within the Church. The Eucharist is the sacrament of communion with one another in the one body of Christ. This was the full meaning of eucharistic *koinonia* in the early church. St. Thomas Aquinas wrote that the Eucharist is the sacrament of the unity of the Church, which results from the fact that many are one in Christ.[40] The Eucharist wasn't meant to be celebrated in isolation or vacuum… because it is a communal.

Radical individualism can lead to an oppressiveness like any cult or totalitarian state.

Human freedom is created and maintained only in the tension between real persons in community with other persons.

A relationship forms our personhood but only if that relationship honors and celebrates both our unity with other persons and our distinction from them. A group that refuses to recognize individual differences and distinctions is a malignant form of community. It will lead to all kinds of evil and pain. But individuals who reject the legitimate claims of community separate themselves from the source of human flourishing.

We are created to develop and celebrate our personal distinctions (and those of others) within loving, healthy

---

40   St. Thomas Aquinas, *The Summa Theologica* (Benziger Bros. edition, 1947).

community. The key is health. This health isn't only for us but for the benefit of others. We are both individual persons and members of community. If we lose either of these foundational realities, we fail to become what we are designed to be.

Isolation happens in worship services where we only hear one another sing (if we can even do that over the volume level of the band) and we only see the backs of heads instead of faces. Do we know what each other thinks or believes? How could we? How do we really know if there are no creeds, prayers, confessions… liturgy? We seem to always want to reinvent the wheel in any context. In search of a new way to do the same thing. What if we could simply lean on the wisdom and experience of those who have gone before us? Look back to learn how to move forward. We could save us some fatigue, anxiety, and frustration. We may even save some time along the way.

Another point of note is our belonging. You belong—no matter how you behave, what you believe, where you go, what you have done—you belong. I can only hope that my wife and I have been intentionally nurturing our three boys with this philosophical notion. No matter where they go and what they do, they belong to us. This is an incredibly important realization.

As we grow and go through life, time will reveal our belonging. We will look back to see where we found deep and meaningful acceptance and kinship. The shadows of doubt and murmurs of lies and suspicion would like to create false narratives that would lead us to believe we have no place to call home, that we will never belong, and that we deserve a life alone in isolation cut off from community and affection.

*Chapter Nineteen*
# Keep Going

How do we reconstruct or expand from here? To allow the process of deconstruction to become a destination instead of a pilgrimage can be tragic. Figuratively, think of reconstructing an engine in a motorbike and then trying to use it to drive to your job. Not only is that absurd, it is dangerous. The process toward reconstruction or reframing actually begins at the moment we commence the reworking of deconstruction. The patient path toward reconstruction can and should be beautiful, but it looks differently from person to person. It's a pilgrimage of rediscovery, discovery, curiosity, healing, and expanding.

Don't be surprised when the subversive craving to recreate a way of faith that is airtight or leakproof becomes a temptation.

Keep going. The more we let go of our illusive need for certainty, the more space and capacity we begin to have for mystery, hope, and faith.

> *And when we come to search for God,*
> *Let us first be robed in night,*
> *Put on the mind of morning*
> *To feel the rush of light*
> *Spread slowly inside*
> *The color and stillness*
> *Of a found world.*
> **—John O'Donohue**, *To Bless the Space Between Us:*
> *A Book of Invocations and Blessings*

Maybe the process of sanctification is a lifelong process. This long, patient process means we have a heightened awareness of God in all things and find all things in God. Holiness doesn't simply happen in isolation. Communion with God and one another assists in the slow lifelong process toward holiness and sanctification.

Holiness is the depth of mystery. With this depth comes awareness, peace, joy, fullness, and a healthy fear (reverence) of the Holy. Community is people wrapped up in a mystery. Community understands through their story, which gives shape and meaning to the mystery. Story honors our common experience.[41]

---

41  Block, Brueggemann, and McKnight, An Other Kingdom: Departing the Consumer Culture.

A *fundamentalist* mind requires explanations and solid answers so much so that it can remain willfully ignorant about history and perspective. Whereas a *liberal* mind may be bent toward an elitist mentality to where objectiveness suffers in the name of open mindedness or agenda ambition. When one ever begins to reform a way of thinking, one may be tempted to swing to the far extreme. Once centered in our convictions and worldview, we should arrive to a resolve of openhandedness and reception. Life is a long, patient process of learning and becoming. With God's help, keep going.

We have a very reduced experience of God. God is present to us, but we are no longer present to God, because we are no longer contemplative. Contemplation can restore our instinct for astonishment.

Telos, in the New Testament, simply means the completion or fulfillment of God's purposes, God's ultimate intention for humanity. In the contours of Scripture, we see that God's intention for humanity is catalyzed by our hands, feet, and minds. Maybe we should think of contextualization as an act of incarnation, of love, of generosity, and space-making with those we are seeking to speak with that is built intellectually and relationally honest. Our environmental awareness, context, brings our actions into a clearer focus.

From exploration and research, it becomes more difficult to blindly accept the actuality of asking Jesus into our heart. It's almost as if you're asking for control in place of Christ. "Where did I put that Jesus?" Christ isn't a possession. Anglo-American Puritans and the evangelicals in the seventeenth and eighteenth centuries began to use the phrase "receive Christ into your heart." John Flavel, a Puritan devotional writer, spoke of those who had heard the Gospel but who would "receive not Christ into their hearts."[42] It seems to be as common for pastors of those centuries to use the phrase to describe an act of devotion in belief. Some would say "receive Christ into their hearts and hold him forth in their lives."

The terminology of "receiving Christ into your heart" became more formalized as a non-Christian's prayer of conversion during the great missionary movement of the nineteenth century. This became more of a mantra for the modern church and for those who believed in the need to make a personal decision to follow Christ, even multiple times if that is what was required. Over the years, we have found the salvation repetition to be problematic, though founded with good intent.

In the 1970s, as children's ministry became more constructed, the leaders looked for simple explanations for children and the need for a decision to follow Christ. Thus, the boom of Vacation Bible School (VBS) across America, where the intent was "winning children to Christ" and to guide them into making "decisions" to ask Jesus into their hearts. This hints at potentially well-intentioned moments of manipulation. Surely, this doesn't negate anyone who has had a genuine moment of devotion as part of a VBS, but authentic presentation and discipleship do not tend to be mutually exclusive. The sinner's prayer, when placed in complete

---

42  Thomas Kidd, "Ask Jesus into Your Heart: A History of the Sinner's Prayer," *Ethics Daily*, https://www.ethicsdaily.com/ask-jesus-into-your-heart-a-history-of-the-sinners-prayer-cms-21668, (April 1, 2014).

theological context, is not a vacuous incantation. The idea that children make such a decision so they can go to heaven instead of the other place is perhaps dangerous and a drastic reduction of the message and hope of the Gospel.

Then there is the idea that means where you begin to walk with Christ, while following His teachings. We should look at what the disciples did—Christ asked them to follow him and they followed him.[43] We know how some of those turned out at the end before Christ was crucified and shortly thereafter. Even so, their devotion was apparent by their actions. Was there ever a recorded time in any of the Gospels to where Christ's disciples asked him into their hearts? The answer is no, that never happened. They were following him on The Way. Our modern constructs have created this concept. It has turned into a reductionist mentality that can potentially be damaging to our children as well as parents.

The way forward for many of us will be new; however, it's actually ancient. There is great wisdom found in looking into the brightness of our past. When we look back, we will discover beauty, pain, tragedy, as well as luminous lifelong lessons. We mustn't forget who we are or, better yet, *whose* we are.

*I stood willingly and gladly in the characters of everything—other people, trees, clouds. And this is what I learned, that the world's otherness is antidote to confusion—that standing within this otherness—the beauty and the mystery of the world, out in the fields or deep inside books—can re-dignify the worst-stung heart.*

---

43  Matthew 4:19 (ESV)

**—Mary Oliver**

Our temptation to cease our meaningful spiritual pilgrimage sometimes comes like waves meeting a sandy shore. There is otherness at play. May your heart be healed, and may you keep going.

> *"But what does it say? "The word is near you, in your mouth and in your heart" (that is, the word of faith that we proclaim); because, if you confess with your mouth that Jesus is Lord and believe in your heart that God raised him from the dead, you will be saved. For with the heart one believes and is justified, and with the mouth one confesses and is saved. For the Scripture says, "Everyone who believes in him will not be put to shame." For there is no distinction between Jew and Greek; for the same Lord is Lord of all, bestowing his riches on all who call on him. For "everyone who calls on the name of the Lord will be saved."* [44]

---

44  Romans 10:8–13 (ESV)

*Chapter Twenty*

# Looking Back for Our Future

Our diet isn't simply what we eat. Our diet includes what we watch, hear, read, breathe, and experience. Our patterns, habits, rhythms, and practices assist our healthy or unhealthy diets.

In full disclosure, the next two chapters are meant to be general trajectories for ancient practices of Christian faith. Those who have come from an evangelical background may find it more enlightening than someone from sacramental circles, and yet many may find the forthcoming monastic description intriguing and helpful.

"The Way" is about the rhythms that set our eyes, heart, and life's postures toward Jesus. At the core, Anglican Spirituality is simple—to know Jesus. From the days of St.

Benedict and St. Ignatius, the accountability, foundations, and proper support were in place through the Church (laity, deacons, priests, bishops). Rooted in orthodoxy, The Way has been embodied through spiritual neo-monastic practices such as Benedictine and Ignatian rhythms. The global Church seems to be reorienting the church in the United States back to the Gospel.

For many, any hint of extraordinary spiritual living is a difficult and inaccessible concept. If you want to dampen a party, just bring up Jesus, conspiracy theories, or the idea of monastic life. Personally, I have always found monasteries and convents fascinating.

There are many versions of monastic orders. Here are just a few:

- Augustinian (354)
- Benedictine (529)
- Dominican (1170)
- Franciscan (1181)
- Ignatian (1491)
- Carmelite (12th century)

In contrast to these ancient orders, look at the modern church, or modern evangelicalism, as approximately 100 years old. Obviously, the modern way of Christian devotion can't be included in a monastic approach, but it may be helpful for us to have a contrast in light of the great orders found throughout the Church's history.

**Ignatian Spirituality**—Sometimes called Jesuit spirituality, Ignatian spirituality was founded on the experiences of the sixteenth century Ignatius of Loyola. Ignatians are the only group to also be called the Society of Jesus.[45] Like all Catholic spirituality, Ignatian spirituality is based on The Way of Jesus (Gospel-based). Anglicans, Methodists, and unaffiliated disciples have all found these practices helpful in their continued spiritual formation and development. Drawing from the teachings of many others before him, Ignatian spirituality goes back to St. Ignatius' Spiritual Exercises whose purpose is "to conquer oneself and to regulate one's life in such a way that no decision is made under the influence of any inordinate attachment." The Exercises are intended to give the person undertaking them a greater degree of freedom from his or her own likes and dislikes, that they may choose based solely on what they discern God's will is for them. Unfortunately, we're inclined to idolatry. We worship created things.

The word "Benedictine" is relatively modern; it scarcely existed before the sixteenth century. It evokes the name of St. Benedict, who lived in the sixth century, together with all those who have been inspired by the Rule of Benedict and associate themselves with the Benedictine spiritual tradition. Since Benedict was a monk, the spirituality based on his rule is fundamentally monastic.

**Benedict's Rule and Spirituality**—Christian monasticism had been in existence for a long time before Benedict wrote

---

45 "The Ignatian Way," *IgnatianSpirituality.com*, https://www.ignatianspirituality.com/what-is-ignatian-spirituality/the-ignatian-way.

his rule. In the East, it dates back to the third century with St. Anthony, and in the West to the fourth century with St. Martin and other founders of monasteries. It was not founded by a particular saint. It appeared little by little wherever the Church took root, a spontaneous manifestation of the Holy Spirit urging Christians to become monks in response to the counsel given by Jesus in the Gospel: "If you would be perfect, go, sell what you possess... follow me..."[46] So, when St. Benedict appeared, monasticism was already implanted in Egypt, Syria, Palestine—the whole East—and in Ireland, Italy, Spain, and Africa in the West. The term was applied to two principal types: the "hermits," who lived alone or in small unorganized groups, and the cenobites, who lived in community. There were also other forms of monastic life, but they were more or less eccentric in comparison with the two main types and sometimes led to abuse. Hence, the spirituality that we find implicit in the Rule of Benedict was dependent in many ways on earlier sources, though he was certainly wise in what he incorporated and what he left behind.

What are the winds in my life? What of those are holy / God winds vs. circumstances, turbulence, consequences, etc.? Ignatius believed that life is a result of choices. An Anglican ethos bears witness—with the same emphasis as the Ignatian Spirituality—to the incarnation of its central doctrine, "in particular its search for wholeness and balance, its desire at once to spread itself outwards in a concern for all human life, and at the same time to turn inwards to explore the heights and depths of God's presence at the heart of human life." The

---

46  Matthew 19:21 (ESV)

Anglican ethos is made up of the predominant conditions and assumptions expressed in feelings, beliefs, and customs that constitute a specific way of proceeding.[47]

**A way to evaluate and refocus:**
- What is my life about? (In general, what is your life about?)
- What do I work for? (Not what you make money for—bringing order out of chaos…)
- What do I love? (Where is your energy, resources, time, etc.?)

OR

- What was my most unfree moment of the day?
- What was my most free moment of the day?
- What are the invitations from both moments?

## Monastic Life

Over the years, I have observed an overwhelming dismissiveness of anything or anyone representing radical devotion. Our culture even uses negative descriptors when speaking of monks, nuns, priests, and bishops. Once I began to study and research monastic life, I became more and more fascinated with it. Over the next section, I will discuss some of my findings in a way that will hopefully illuminate aspects to these deep means of devotion.

47 Paolo Gamberini, *Ignatian Spirituality and Anglican Ethos: A Family Resemblance*, https://www.academia.edu/21801036/ignatian_spirituality_and_anglican_ethos_a_family_resemblance_.

**Monastic Spirituality**—Monastic existence is a form of spiritual and religious life for ministerial and personal devotion purposes. It is specified solely by a commitment to God sanctioned by public vows. Tradition assigns no other end to monastic life than to "seek God" or "to live for God alone," an ideal that can be achieved only by a life of conversion, communion, and prayer.

The first and fundamental manifestation of such a vocation is a real separation from many aspects of the outside world. All monks are by definition "solitaries," for this is the original meaning of their name, which comes from the Greek word *monachos*, derived from *monos*, to which corresponds the Latin *solus* (alone). The second characteristic of the monastic vocation is that it demands a life of which a privileged part is given to prayer.

Personal or private prayer is traditionally exercised under the form of meditative reading of Holy Scripture and of authors who explain and reflect on it, according to the three phases designated by the words "reading" (*lectio*), "meditation" (*meditatio*), and "prayer" (*oratio* or *contemplatio*). In monastic life, public prayer is only one observance among those which help the monk seek God. It is not one of the distinguishing characteristics of early monastic life. Only in later centuries and especially since the nineteenth century has it occupied a more important place in monastic life than in the observance of the majority of non-monastic religious congregations, with the consequence that it is usually considered a special feature of monastic life and spirituality.

Transformation is the key. At our parish, we acknowledge the desire to cooperate with God in the transformations of our souls. It is the work of the Holy Spirit. Practices, exercises, and rhythms can help us to be open to this change. We can know Jesus at three places: Manger, Cross, and Empty Tomb. Obviously, there are more places, but we're going to look at these.

- **Manger:** Do you feel hopeless or alone? Look to the Manger for the willingness of God to send his Son to be God with us.
- **Cross:** Do you need a sense of humility against your pride? Look to the sacrifice of Christ.
- **Empty Tomb:** Do you battle with depression or defeat? Look to the resurrection for a bigger picture that God has made a way to defeat death and made a way when there seemed to be no way.

## General Principles

According to Hans Urs von Balthasar, "choice" is the center of Spiritual Exercises. The original objective was the question of the choice of a state of life. After a time of practicing these exercises, many people tend to make major life choices—life-changing choices. Disciplines are not about enabling God to love me more… God is God loving. Disciplines are acts and rhythms of devotion.

The Ignatian process of making good decisions acknowledges that decisions are often between two goods, understanding that the better good, or "the more" (Latin: *magis*), is what we instinctively want, and what God wants for us. "In all things, to love and to serve" (Spanish: "*en todo amar y servir*") was a motto of St. Ignatius, who wanted to "be like St. Francis and St. Dominic," though better. Everything has purpose, though there can be a dissonance within our faith.

**St. Ignatius of Loyola**—"A man who gave the first place of his life to God," said Benedict XVI. Ignatius stressed that "Man is created to praise, reverence, and serve God Our Lord and by this means to save his soul." This is the "First Principle and Foundation" of the Exercises. Ignatius declares: "The goal of our life is to live with God forever. God who loves us, gave us life. Our own response of love allows God's life to flow into us without limit... Our only desire and our one choice should be this: 'I want, and I choose what better leads to the deepening of God's life in me.'"

**Union with Jesus:** Ignatius emphasized an ardent love for the Savior. In his month-long Exercises, he devoted the last three weeks to the contemplation of Jesus: from infancy and public ministry, to his passion, and lastly his risen life. To achieve empathy with Jesus and a closer following of him, Ignatius proposed a form of contemplation that he called "application of the senses" to the scenes in the life of Jesus. The Spiritual Exercises sum this up in a prayer that I may "love him more and follow him more closely." There is a considerable emphasis on the emotions in Ignatius' methods, and a call for one to be sensitive to emotional movements.

**Self-awareness:** In a broad scope, self-awareness enables grounding, as we discussed earlier in the book. This affects not only us individually, but those around us. After time, we can tend to be less insecure, difficult, and petty while being more confident, harmonious, and peaceful. We look to the Enneagram for insight and assessment. Ignatius recommends the twice-daily Examen (examination).

This is a guided method of prayerfully reviewing the events of the day, to awaken one's inner sensitivity to one's own actions, desires, and spiritual state through each moment reviewed. The goals are to see where God is challenging the person to change and to grow, where God is calling the person to deeper reflection (especially apt when discerning if one has a Jesuit vocation in life), to where sinful or imperfect attitudes or blind spots are found. The general Examen, often at the end of the day, is, as the name implies, a general review. The particular Examen, often in the middle of the day, focuses on a particular fault—identified by the person—to be worked upon in the course of some days or weeks. Since the 1970s, there have been numerous in-depth studies and adaptations of the Examen to contemporary needs. This is explained below under the title "Examen of Consciousness."

**Spiritual direction:** Meditation and contemplation and, for instance, the aforementioned Examen, are best guided, Ignatius says, by an experienced person. Jesuits, and those following Ignatian spirituality, meet with their spiritual director (traditionally a priest, though in recent years many laypersons have undertaken this role) on a regular basis (weekly or monthly) to discuss the fruits of their prayer life and be offered guidance. Ignatius sees the director as someone who can rein in impulsiveness or excesses, goad the complacent, and keep people honest with themselves.

But the director should not so much explain but simply present the exercises, to not get in the way of God who "communicates himself with the well-disposed person." If the director is a priest, spiritual direction may or may not be connected with the Sacrament of Reconciliation.

**Effective love:** The founder of the Society of Jesus emphasized effective love (love shown in deeds) over affective love (love based on feelings). He usually ended his most important letters with "I implore God to grant us all the grace to know His holy will and to accomplish it perfectly." This love, which leads us to a perfect correspondence with God's will, demands self-sacrifice—renunciation of personal feelings and preferences. This is expressed in Ignatius' prayer in the last exercise of his Spiritual Exercises, which remains popular among Jesuits: "Take Lord and receive, all my liberty."

**Detachment:** Where Francis of Assisi's concept of poverty emphasized the spiritual benefits of simplicity and dependency, Ignatius emphasized detachment, or "indifference." This figures prominently into what Ignatius called the "First Principle and Foundation" of the Exercises. For Ignatius, whether one was rich or poor, healthy or sick, in an assignment one enjoyed or one didn't, was comfortable in a culture or not, etc., should be a matter of spiritual indifference—a modern phrasing might put it as serene acceptance. Hence, a Jesuit (or one following Ignatian spirituality) placed in a comfortable, wealthy neighborhood should continue to live the Gospel life without anxiety or possessiveness, and if plucked from that situation to be placed in a poor area and subjected to hardships should, with a sense of spiritual joy, accept that as well, looking only to do God's will.

## Prayer and Efforts of Self-Conquest

Ignatius' book *The Spiritual Exercises* is the fruit of months of prayer. Prayer, in Ignatian spirituality, is fundamental since it was at the foundation of Jesus' life, but it does not dispense from "helping oneself," a phrase frequently used by Ignatius. Thus, he also speaks of mortification and of amendment.

St. Ignatius counseled people to receive the Eucharistic bread more often and, from the order's earliest days, the Jesuits were promoters of "frequent communion." It should be noted that it was the custom for many Catholics at that time to receive Holy Communion perhaps once or twice a year, out of what Catholic theologians considered an exaggerated respect for the sacrament. Ignatius and others advocated receiving the sacrament even weekly, emphasizing Holy Communion not as reward but as spiritual food. By the time of Pope St. Pius X (1903–1914), "frequent communion" had come to mean weekly, even daily reception. Though many believe that more frequent participation can possibly lead to less of a meaningful acknowledgement, it typically proves to be deeper and formative.

**Zeal for souls:** The purpose of the Society of Jesus, says the Summary of the Constitutions, is "not only to apply oneself to one's own salvation and to perfection with the help of divine grace, but to employ all one's strength for the salvation and perfection of one's neighbor."

**Finding God in all things:** The vision that Ignatius places at the beginning of the Exercises keeps sight of both the Creator and the creature, the One and the other swept along in the same movement of love. In it, God offers himself to humankind in an absolute way through the Son, and humankind responds in an absolute way by a total self-donation.

There is no longer sacred or profane, natural or supernatural, mortification or prayer—because it is one and the same Spirit who brings it about that the Christian will see and "love God in all things—and all things in God." Hence, Jesuits have always been active in the graphic and dramatic arts, literature, and the sciences.

**Examen of Consciousness:** The Examen of Consciousness is a simple prayer directed toward developing a spiritual sensitivity to the special ways God approaches, invites, and calls. Ignatius recommends that the Examen be done at least twice, and suggests five points of prayer with a proper posture:

1. Recalling that one is in the presence of God
2. Thanking God for all the blessings one has received
3. Examining how one has lived the day
4. Asking God for forgiveness
5. Resolution and offering a prayer of hopeful recommitment

It is important, however, that you feel free to structure the Examen in a way that is personally most helpful. There is no right way to do it; nor is there a need to go through all of the five points each time. You might, for instance, find yourself spending the entire time on only one or two points. The basic rule is: Go wherever God draws you. And this touches upon an important point: the Examen of Consciousness is primarily a time of prayer; it is "being with God." It focuses on your consciousness of God, not necessarily your conscience regarding sins and mistakes.

**Discernment:** Discernment is rooted in the understanding that God is ever at work in one's life, "inviting, directing, guiding, and drawing" one "into the fullness of life." Its central action is reflection on the ordinary events of one's life. It presupposes an ability to reflect, a habit of personal prayer, self-knowledge, knowledge of one's deepest desires, and openness to God's direction and guidance. Discernment is a prayerful "pondering" or "mulling over" the choices a person wishes to consider. In discernment, the person's focus should be on a quiet attentiveness to God and sensing rather than thinking. The goal is to understand the choices in one's heart, to see them, as it were, as God might see them. In one sense, there is no limit to how long one might wish to continue in this. Discernment is a repetitive process yet, as the person continues, some choices should have their own accord fall by the wayside while others should gain clarity and focus. It is a process that should move inexorably toward a decision.

**Service and humility:** Ignatius emphasized the active expression of God's love in life and the need to be self-forgetful in humility. Part of Jesuit formation is the undertaking of service specifically to the poor and sick in the most humble of ways: Ignatius wanted Jesuits in training to serve part of their time as novices and in Tertianship as the equivalent of orderlies in hospitals, for instance, emptying bedpans and washing patients, to learn humility and loving service. Jesuit educational institutions often adopt mottoes and mission statements that include the idea of making students "men and women for others," and the like.

## Aspects of Benedictine Spirituality

The Rule of Benedict opens with the word "listen" (Spanish: *ausculta*). This is the key to Benedict's whole spiritual teaching. A monk should be above all a good listener. One of the primary functions of the various monastic structures is to provide conditions in which the monks can concentrate on learning the art of listening.

Monks are to listen "to the precepts of the master" but their primary and ultimate master is God. It is only in a secondary sense that Benedict himself, speaking through the Rule, and the abbot of the community, are masters. The whole spiritual life of the monk consists of listening to God by "inclining the ear of the heart." This listening is not merely an intellectual or rational activity; it is intuitive, springing from the very core of the monk's being where he is most open to God and most open to the word of life that God speaks. God speaks to the monk through Christ, but the monk is called to see Christ not only in the superior but also in the guests, in the sick, in the young, and in the old. In a very special way, God speaks through the Scriptures, through the liturgy of the hours (Opus Dei), and through personal prayer. This means that the monk must be very quiet and still within himself, but also very alert and attentive, if the word of God is to resonate properly within his innermost depths so that he is enlightened and nourished by it.[48]

Benedict calls the monastery a "school" because it is the place where the monk is to be taught by God. This invitation to listen came to Benedict from the heart of the Old and New Testament traditions. The monk's listening is to be modeled after the prayer of Jesus, who spent long hours listening and was attentive in the presence of his heavenly Father.

Humility is also a dominant theme in Benedictine spirituality; in fact, it is closely related to contemplation. It is humility that takes the monk beyond the myth of his own grandeur to the grandeur of God. If he gets the grandeur of God in place, he is apt to get the rest of monastic life in place too. Humility enables the monk to stand in awe before the world and to receive the gifts of God and others. In Benedict's Rule, humility is not the same as humiliations, for humiliations degrade the person. The Rule is marked by a strong sense of the individual monk's personal worth and dignity. Humility is the ability to recognize one's rightful place in the universe and to see oneself as a mysterious combination of strengths and weaknesses. The Rule invites the monk to recognize the presence of God in his life, a presence that is not gained or won or achieved but instead is simply given.

Benedict's community might well be called a formation community in which all, including the abbot and other superiors in the community, are in the process of being formed throughout their lives into the likeness of Christ by attentive listening to the word of God, and a loving response to that word

---

48   St. Benedict, *The Rule of Saint Benedict* (Vintage, 1998).

mediated into the life of the community by Christ's own offer of friendship through the communication of the Holy Spirit. Hence, conversion to Christ and response to his love through the power of the Holy Spirit are the goals of obedience. It is likewise through that response that one becomes free to be and develop as the person one is called to be. The ideal of this pattern of conversion is meant to be incarnated in a special way for the community in the abbot, who is expected to be a symbolic center exercising a centripetal force that draws individuals into a truly Christian community of life for God and others in Jesus Christ through the power of the Holy Spirit.

Simplicity of life and a sense of stewardship are also characteristics of Benedictine spirituality. The monk is called to discern how the Benedictine tradition speaks to the basic human condition, often characterized by blindness and greed. At the heart of his contemplative tradition are values directly opposed to blindness, materialism, and greed. Poverty of spirit, simplicity, sharing and giving, self-denial prompted by love, freedom of heart, gratitude, care for persons, and sound judgment with regard to created things should proceed from exposure to God in prayer. Certainly the Rule does not see material privation as an end in itself; it is in no way part of the Benedictine tradition to assess everything economically by materialistic standards or to override aesthetic or other values for the sake of cheapness or squalor, for such a mentality narrows the monk's horizons and even creates those very evils accompanying destitution, which all Christians have a duty to banish from the earth. Benedictine simplicity of life is understood properly with the reality of Christ and his mission in mind. It is rooted in faith, and like

Christ's own simplicity of life must be an outward expression of trustful dependence on God.[49]

## The Seven Pillars of Benedictine Spirituality[50]

### Community

It is a lifestyle of learning to relate and respond to God through events and people one encounters in daily life. In community, we seek the mystery of God through and in contemplation. The Benedictine spiritual disciplines include common prayer, serving God though hospitality and mutual service, conversion of life, relationships, and solitude. Our energy naturally flows toward others. Relationships direct us toward God. As St. Benedict states, "You cannot do life alone."

### Hospitality

Chapter 53 of *The Rule of St. Benedict* states that all guests who present themselves are to be welcomed as Christ. It is marked by embracing every human as sacred and every life as holy ground. In this act of faith, equal dignity of all is assumed. Solitude and silence are the liberating force that frees the individual soul to be with God. Patience, discipline, and waiting are key elements necessary to cultivate the art of practicing silence and solitude. In "waiting," we listen to the other and seek a deeper meaning

---

49    Patrick Barry, Richard Yeo and Kathleen Norris, *Wisdom from the Monastery: The Rule of St. Benedict for Everyday Life*, (Liturgical Press, 2006).

50    "The Seven Pillars of Benedictine Spirituality," *Benet Hill Monastery*, https://benethillmonastery.com/vocations/the-seven-pillars-of-benedictine-spirituality.

and understanding of God in our life. Benedictine spirituality is about listening to the other attentively; this action directs us toward wholeness because we let the other into our life. It means we have the positive intention to listen to the other, to hear God's voice in that person.

### Humility

It is to be authentic before God. It is facing the truth that we are humus, that stuff in which the earth is made, and our hearts recognize and honor our place in the universe. God is God and we are not! It is to recognize the presence of God in our lives through contemplation. In this contemplative stance, we journey to wholeness to create balance of mind, body, spirit, and heart. It calls us to remember the God within so we can recognize the gifts of others, the earth, and all creatures. We must continually surrender to God's power in our life and in the lives of those around us.

### Reverence

It is an attitude in faith that we honor the Christ in the other, the mystery and awe of God in our lives. It is the holding sacred the precious encounters in human relationship, our earth partnership, and of all creation. It is to stand in the spiral mystery of faith wrapped in God's presence.

### Stewardship/Partnership

We are one with the earth, not power over the earth. This lived gratitude allows us to use our human and earthly resources wisely. It holds all creation as sacred and holy.

## *Integration*

It is the divine dance to embrace the Benedictine spiritual disciplines to live out of that relationship with our God from our heart place. In the center of our being dwells a heart that is one, a stranger to division, forever it whispers *I am already within you: Believe in me*! It is the undivided heart that leads the divine dance to connect the mind, body, and spirit to universal harmony and peace.

## *Discernment*

To discern is to sort out, in the light of the whole, that which is God. It is the gift of sight to sort our thoughts to see if they are of God. It is to find the will of God in the circumstances of daily living. It is turning toward God in those little moments in our lived ordinariness, which we chose, to partnership with God. Discernment is a sorting process that moves issues, questions, and concerns out of the realm of thoughts, feelings, emotions, and body sensations away from self-will to a disposition of complete surrender to the will of God in our choices. "Discernment is living life prayerfully, bringing oneself to God honestly and completely as possible, seeking God's guidance as openly as possible, and then in faith, responding as fully as possible."[51]

> *There's something about the rhythm of walking, how, after about an hour and a half, the mind and body can't help getting in sync.*
>
> **—Bjork**

---

51 Gerald May, *Addiction and Grace* (HarperOne, 2007).

## The Examen

The Examen of Consciousness is a simple prayer directed toward developing a spiritual sensitivity to the special ways God approaches, invites, and calls.

*Begin:*

Assume a posture of stillness and reverent relaxation.

- Be aware that God is with you.
- Be thankful to God for blessings.
- Examine how you have lived the day.
- Confess sin and ask God for forgiveness.
- Resolve and offer prayer of hopeful devotion.

*Finish:*

- Resolve posture of stillness and reverent relaxation.

It is important, however, that the person feels free to structure the Examen in a way that is personally most helpful. There is no right way to do it, nor is there a need to go through all of the five points each time. A person might, for instance, find oneself spending the entire time on only one or two points. The basic rule is: Go wherever God draws you.

And this touches upon an important point: the Examen of Consciousness is primarily *a time of prayer; it is a "being with God." It focuses on one's consciousness of God, not necessarily one's conscience regarding sins and mistakes.*[52]

---

52 Mark E. Thibodeaux, SJ, *Reimagining the Ignatian Examen* (Loyola Press, 2015).

*Chapter Twenty-One*
# The Canterbury Path

For the majority of my forty-something years, I have intentionally stayed at arm's length and even cringed at the thought of affiliating myself with a specific religious denomination. Most of this stems from the nature of ministry I have served during my years of travels and staffing. Maybe it's been the artist in me saying, "Don't label me. I mean, I'm just following Jesus." Or maybe (probably) most of the affiliated religious streams have been known more for what they stand against instead of what they stand for.

Over the past fifteen years, there has been more and more gravity compelling me toward ancient practices rooted in the rich history of Early Church. From the overexposure to the attraction model of church, I eventually became fatigued with re-inventing the wheel week after week and expecting magical results from a production / presentation. A couple of my close friends have been forthcoming enough to ask if any of my jadedness or cynicism has played into my frustration of the evangelical mega-church model. That may be true, but I have realized something very significant in the process—there is a difference between running away from something and being compelled toward something.

With a membership estimated at around eighty-five million members, the Anglican Communion is the third largest Christian communion in the world, after the Catholic Church and the Eastern Orthodox Churches. The Anglican Church has and always will have its tensions in many varieties, but that will be found in any human endeavor. For my family and I, we have had a sense of coming home with Anglicanism.

We have had many friends who support us along the way and curiosity continues to grow. Sacramental hunger lies within each of us, though it may reveal itself in different ways. We are wired to be experiential. In liturgical spaces, everything becomes meaningful and symbolic. In the offering up of the bread and wine, we see the offering up of the wheat and grain and fruits of the earth, and God gives them back in a sanctified form. Though it may seem to "work" for some, many of us are thirsty for meaning that goes deeper than the brand with a thirty-minute concert and a forty-five-minute motivational speech.

We should lean into our ache for sacramentality. Each year, there have been some liturgical conversations and practices, especially with Holy Eucharist. Many artists, and even pragmatists, tend to resonate with these types of practices due to the meaningful history, anchoring, and lack of personality-centricity. No, it's not without fault and issues because there is human involvement.

As I continue to have conversations with some of my evangelical friends, the questions continue to come in regard to the sacramental ways. The levels of curiosity outweigh misconceptions. The beautiful thing is there are many on the path toward a more rooted, anchored, and rich tradition with liturgical and ancient forms. The liturgy is centering, robust, and moving and, contrary to popular belief, it is passionate, beautiful, meaningful, and vibrant. The music tends to be diverse, poetic, and spirited.

Anglican Christianity is rooted in the ancient faith and practice of the first century church, tracing its history through missionaries to the British Isles and the development of Celtic Christianity early in the first millennium A.D.

Driven by a missionary focus, Anglicanism has mostly been about the work of making disciples for centuries and has expanded into a global expression. Its essential statement of faith is expressed in both the Nicene and Apostles' Creeds. It has received the English Book of Common Prayer, originally published in 1549, as its beautiful liturgical worship resource.

Anglicanism seeks to embrace the foundation of the Apostles and early Church Fathers in our worship and practice. As we observe Via Media, which is Latin for the "middle path," we have many opportunities to facilitate conversations within culture from each side. Anglicans are strategically positioned to be workers of peace, reason, and cultural change. We are not the first on this journey of faith, and we will not be the last. Therefore, we seek to embrace those elements of worship and theology that clearly affirm the truths of the Gospel while continuing to seek fresh ways in which that truth can be expressed in our current time.

The desire of the early Anglican reformers of the official Anglican Church was to stay true to the ancient traditions of the early church but in a way that was accessible to the people of sixteenth century England. So, at the heart of Anglican Christianity is a desire to be simultaneously *rooted and relevant, ancient and modern, traditional and innovative.* Nowhere is this more plainly seen than in the Book of Common Prayer (BCP). In the Anglican Communion, you will find a diverse network of churches, practices, and styles, yet all connected with the BCP.

Originally written in 1549 by Thomas Cranmer, the Prayer Book revolutionized the life and worship of the Church. Cranmer's BCP was a brilliant innovation that brought new life and meaning to the ancient worship traditions of the church, because, for the first time, they were simplified (made user friendly) and written in the language of the people rather than in Latin.

The BCP is also thoroughly infused with Scripture references from beginning to end as Cranmer had a deep conviction in the transforming power of God's written word.

As the Eastern Orthodox Church began the path of the first Christian church, it is possible that the new Anglican church is going to serve as the "Western Orthodox Church." Immersed in the culture of "the West," yet providing a counter-cultural way of living our ancient faith may help provide North America with an orthodox way forward. Over the next forty to sixty years it will be interesting to see what aspect Anglicanism will serve in our society.

Anglicanism and its practices may not be for everyone. It certainly requires our collective effort in the work of the Kingdom Come and will being done here on earth as it is in heaven. There is much to be done and many ways to do it. We need more ecumenical bridge-building opportunities with less divisive fragmenting within the Church. May we not continue to fear (or judge) what we don't understand.

A few points of interest:

1. This decision is really more personal than it is public (yes, it's ironic that I'm doing a post about it).
2. It is deepening everything that I have done in my church and musical past.
3. Though much of religion can be stifling, my hope for the Church has never been brighter. I believe that much of the Anglican practice is what will help bring balance and further movement to the Church as a whole.

The Anglican Way has been a model of rhythm, process, and temperance for centuries before it became the Anglican Church. Celtic Spirituality was a process of belonging before believing. Arguably, since the late third, early fourth century, Christianity made its way to the British Isles and brought a non-Roman expression approach to discipleship and devotion. The Anglican Way isn't the only way, but it is Another Way.

## Active Streams

The Three Streams approach to living a life with sacred rhythms includes an active focus on Scripture, Sacrament, and Spirit. There are many meaningful layers to the Three Streams practice. A practical approach to these streams can be:

- Daily Office (daily / weekly readings)
- Private Devotion (the way you live when no one else is looking)
- Holy Communion (both personal and collective worship)

This past year, a prominent evangelical teacher and author, Beth Moore, swung for the fence by tweeting "if church = grading the pastor and worship team on how good the show is, let's save ourselves the trouble of Bibles and bring popcorn and Coke."

With this in mind, when we pursue our religious spectacles and productions, that will only ever make sense to us when we find ourselves disenchanted and lacking wonder. "Our way" of church has come unhinged over the years. In order to correctively move forward, we must look back to the early ancient Church of Pentecost.

The spectacle model church is continuing to cultivate a more consumer-driven individualism looking no different from the frayed culture around us. Being light-bearing images of our Maker isn't an alternative relativism based on popular culture. That has been found to be shallow, unsustainable, and death-bearing.

*Chapter Twenty-Two*

# A Way Forward

*For Jesus, there are no countries to be conquered, no ideologies to be imposed, no people to be dominated. There are only children, women and men to be loved.*

**—Henri Nouwen**

There will always be another way forward. Some are more healthy, peaceful, and robust than others. One of the most important and helpful attributes we can develop over time is discernment. A large portion of discernment comes from our experiences. Reflection offers a retrospective observation, so we can truly examine how everything may connect along our way. Reflection can be a birthplace of discernment, a space of awareness and awakening.

Some of us may believe the only way forward is a renouncing, exit, or unraveling of our faith. Many more than likely will endeavor a quiet life of belief in God outside of the walls of the Church. With no loud or turbulent exit of the church buildings, many of you will intentionally begin to engage with family, friends, and nature on Sundays in lieu of an organized community of faith. From a seasonal perspective, that may be the proper action to enable a health detox or palate cleanser, if you will. There is a way forward, however.

I meet with evangelical pastors / staff on a weekly basis. Most are nearing the end of their "professional" ministry life, looking for another way forward. Their discontent goes far deeper than simple philosophical differences or hurt feelings. Most of them are nomads, caught in a place they no longer belong, but once called home. If you are one of these wonderful humans, I would like to wish you the deepest peace of God. Peace in the darkest portions of your soul—peace that surely passes all possible understanding.

Prayerfully and patiently seek out a confessor. This will come with confidence, non-disclosure, and trust. Regardless of our tradition or bias, a confessor will serve as a safe place to confess trappings, failings, and temptations. Without a confessor, we will pretend to operate in health while unknowingly (or knowingly) living with unhealthy patterns and habits.

A good portion of friends (old and new) whom I speak with each week are at interesting points on their spiritual pilgrimage. From the process of deconstruction to reconstruction, from apathy and pain to thriving and loving.

There are some trendy voices who resonate with us due to their Gnosticism. All of us will resonate with a gnostic message at some point. When we give space to patently process any level of enlightenment, we will begin to see that Christ remains centric to our being. I would dare say that when Jesus is revealed to be who Christ truly is, our faith becomes recalibrated to the true self.

Voices encouraging transcendence beyond Christ to subversively create new "truths" will eventually become unhealthy humanism at its best and toxic, hopeless individualism at its worst. Unfortunately, this can be weaponized. Any layer to a weaponized faith is no faith at all. It may be easier for us to see how the American church has used a weaponized philosophy to impose its will on a society that simply can't see past the hypocrisy of its people.

In *Prayer: Our Deepest Longing*, Ronald Rolheiser said, "At the end of the day, we expect that God is disappointed with us and will greet us with a frown. The tragedy and sadness here is that we avoid God when we are most in need of love and acceptance. Because we think God is disappointed in us, especially at those times when we are disappointed in ourselves, we fail to meet the one person, the one love, and the one energy—God—that actually understands us, accepts us, delights in us, and is eager to smile at us."

There is no substitute for the retention potential of self-discovery. That is to say, the process of finding something out on your own. A symptom of the illness of hurry in our life is quick knowledge.[53] Expedited, or shortcut information is only one dimensional. Something worth knowing is something worth discovering. The ancient text of Scripture is no different.

We are reading commentary or listening to podcasts rather than doing our own exploration. Sure, that may save us time, but can potentially misinform or deform us in the process. Gravitating toward a trusted voice isn't a bad motive, necessarily. When we exclusively trust commentary, we don't test of research our sources. There is no substitute for our personal findings. After unearthing substance, we can then reference the commentary we trust but mustn't be surprised when we differ from time to time.

We have a deep need to embrace the "wilderness" once again. In the Way of Jesus, we see space to confront our demons, work out our faith, as well as practice reflection, solitude, stillness, and silence. These rhythms will most certainly change our way of life over time. They have for many and will for anyone who follows.

Some points of practice to enable peace, stillness, and spiritual health:

1. When possible, befriend silence.
2. Don't be afraid to normalize "boredom."
3. Pray prayers of those who have gone before us.
4. Begin to embrace the idea of trust again.

---

53  Rosemary Sword and Philip Zimbardo, "Hurry Sickness," *Psychology Today*, https://www.psychologytoday.com/us/blog/the-time-cure/201302/hurry-sickness, (February 9, 2013).

The word "follow" in the Greek indicates "cling to" or imitate. We mustn't cling to or imitate celebrities, be it Christian or not. This is a part of the way forward: Eventually arriving at centering points of belief and understanding stir a deeper communion while lessening our apprehensions of study and exegesis. Many souls have left an institutional faith and will continue to do so, many in search of their version of Christ. I'm coming to realize that many of them genuinely love Jesus and are devoted on some level, but something in their church experience has left them traumatized hurt and damaged. There seems to be more and more opportunity for people to try to find their way to face outside of the church's walls.

Honestly, I don't find myself tempted to try to move them back into a church or encourage them to find their way back into a church community, though it may be a helpful direction. As James writes in his first chapter, I hope to quick to listen, slow to speak and hear what they're saying and not saying or unable to express. This could help us all with a way forward.

Wherever you are on the pilgrimage, please be encouraged that you are not alone, not forgotten, nor are you frowned upon. God isn't displeased by your doubt, journey, or disbelief. Keep walking, crawling, going. Allow your disgust, frustration, and hurt to turn and heal over time. It's a long and patient path. Don't believe anyone who says differently.

Regardless of your beliefs, how inadequate you may think you are, or how complete you feel you are, this is true: you are a beloved daughter or son of I AM.

# A Benediction

My sisters and brothers, when you are confronted with your own inadequacy, may you be reminded that Jesus is enough.

When you are confronted with your own weakness, may you find endurance and strength in Christ.

When you are confronted with discontent and frustration, may you rest in the peace of Jesus.

When you are confronted with your past and all of the ways that you aren't good enough, may you rest in your present and your future and all of the ways that Jesus is good enough.

When you are confronted with despair, may you have the hope of Christ.

When anxiety and worry's riptide attempt to pull you under, may the anchor of Jesus hold you steadfast.

When you seek Holy presence, may you find yourself already immersed in His pervasive presence and peace.

In the stillness, may you truly come to sense that in Jesus you are a new creation.

May the peace of our God be with you and may you share this peace with everyone you meet. To the glory of the Father, and to the Son, and to the Holy Spirit. As it was in the beginning, is now, and will be forever. Amen.

# Epilogue

Several months ago, while in San Antonio, Texas, I started one morning in a crowded coffee shop. My time was limited, and my temperament was less than affable. I was attempting to be focused and efficient, until someone's unwelcomed turbulence agitated the space.

Enter the agitator—a Hispanic-American female in her late forties, descending at the two-top next to me. In tow, her dark cloud of irritability and contempt. I swear the brilliant morning sun that was blaring through the front windows disappeared with her presence. Her life was obviously not what she or any of us would have wanted it to be.

My insistent concentration began to dissipate after five minutes of her speaking to herself out loud. This morning had quickly transitioned to a lesson and opportunity to embody what I had been so diligently writing about for the past few years. A pursuit of peace and spiritual health will always present moments of potential presence, help, and kindness.

We'll say her name is Francis, after St. Francis of Assisi, due to the birds tweeting outside the coffee shop windows. Francis had carried her burdens into the shop like a thick winter sweater. She may not have even realized its weight at this point. Francis was in desperate need of assistance. Her life was consuming her and everyone around her.

As I noticed the time, I began to close my computer and store it in my bag. Before heading outside to meet my ride, I took a deep breath and prayed a portion of the Confession, "I confess that I have sinned against you in thought, word, and deed, by what I have done, and by what I have left undone… I have not loved my neighbor as myself…"

"Please excuse me," I said to her as I shifted my bag over my head. "I hope you don't think this is too odd, but before I leave, I want to offer you peace." Her eyes slowed for the first time that morning. "What is that, you said?" she replied. "In my spiritual tradition, we offer one another peace each Sunday, with a handshake and direct eye contact, and we pass what peace we have along. May I?" "Okay," she said. I held my hand out as she apprehensively received it; I said, "May the peace of our Great God be with you always."

I simply smiled and as I began to walk outside, I noticed something that may have a profound mark on me for some time. Tears began to fill Francis' eyes and the massive dark cloud scattered. She produced a light smile, wiped her eyes and said,

"I haven't had anyone offer me peace since I was a little girl. I grew up going to Catholic mass every week. Thank you, sir."

The moment Francis walked into the shop, I made a choice to ignore her problems, and by the time I left, I chose to shoulder a portion of her unknown cloud. There was no extra weight, stress, or frustration thereafter. I had received as much peace as I had shared.

# About the Author

Chad E. Jarnagin is a former baseball player, an ordained priest in the Anglican Communion, an artist, and a writer. He is a contemplative and passionate dreamer. An Enneagram Type 5 with an almost equal 4-Wing.

Chad spent approximately twenty years as a touring musician. He continues to co-write and play music on occasion. He served as a member of the President's Advisory Council on Faith-Based and Neighborhood Partnerships (2002-2007).

He is the founding rector of Luminous Parish, an Anglican Mission to Nashville | Franklin, Tennessee.

Chad grew up around Cincinnati, Ohio, and has lived in the Nashville area for over twenty years. He and his wife, Jennifer, have three fun and creative boys.

Fr. Chad schedules a limited number of events for speaking, music, retreat guide, and caring for staffs of churches and organizations using the wisdom of the Enneagram.

Please go to ChadJarnagin.com for more information.

# References

## Articles

Anderson, G. Oscar. "Loneliness Among Older Adults: A National Survey of Adults 45+." Washington, DC: AARP Research, September 2010. https://assets.aarp.org/rgcenter/general/loneliness_2010.pdf

Hutson, Matthew. "People Prefer Electric Shocks to Being Alone with Their Thoughts." *The Atlantic*. July 3, 2014. https://www.theatlantic.com/health/archive/2014/07/people-prefer-electric-shocks-to-being-alone-with-their-thoughts/373936/ (accessed December 1, 2018).

Kreider, Tim. "The 'Busy' Trap." *The New York Times*. June 30, 2012. https://opinionator.blogs.nytimes.com/2012/06/30/the-busy-trap (accessed December 1, 2018).

Rohr, Richard. "Life on the Edge: Understanding the Prophetic Position." *HuffPost*. March 19, 2011. https://www.huffingtonpost.com/fr-richard-rohr/on-the-edge-of-the-inside_b_829253.html

Schiffman, Richard. "Why People Who Pray Are Healthier Than Those Who Don't." *HuffPost*. March 19, 2012. https://www.huffingtonpost.com/entry/why-people-who-pray-are-heathier_b_1197313 (accessed December 1, 2018).

Sword, Zimbardo. Hurry Sickness. *Psychology Today*, February 9, 2013. https://www.psychologytoday.com/us/blog/the-time-cure/201302/hurry-sickness

Ware, Kallistos. "Jesus Prayer–Unification." https://www.orthodoxprayer.org/Articles_files/Ware-5%20Unification.html

## Books

Backhouse, Robert. *A Feast of Anglican Spirituality*. Canterbury Press, 2012.

Barry, Patrick, Richard Yeo, and Kathleen Norris. *Wisdom from the Monastery: The Rule of St. Benedict for Everyday Life*. Liturgical Press, 2006.

Barry, William A., SJ. *Finding God in All Things*. Ave Maria Press, 1991.

Block, Peter and Walter Brueggemann and John McKnight. *An Other Kingdom*. Wiley, 2014.

Brown Taylor, Barbara. *Leaving Church: A Memoir of Faith*. HarperOne, 2007.

Brown Taylor, Barbara. *Learning to Walk in the Dark.*
HarperOne, 2014.

Chittister, Joan, OSB. *Wisdom Distilled from the Daily.* Harper
Collins. 1991.

Derkse, Wil. *The Rule of Benedict for Beginners: Spirituality for
Daily Life.* Liturgical Press, 2003.

Heschel, Abraham. *The Sabbath.* Farrar Straus Giroux, 2005.

Kavanaugh, John F. *Following Christ in a Consumer Society.*
Orbis Books, 2006.

Lamott, Anne. *Bird by Bird.* Anchor Books, 1995.

May, Gerald. *Addiction and Grace.* Harper Collins, 1988.

Merton, Thomas. *Contemplative Prayer.* Herder and Herder,
1969.

Merton, Thomas. *A Life in Letters: The Essential Collection.*
HarperOne, 2008.

Oliver, Mary. "Sometimes."

Palmer, Parker J. *Let Your Life Speak: Listening for the Voice of
Vocation.* Jossey-Bass, 1999.

Pressfield, Steve. *The War of Art.* Grand Central Press, 2002.

Rohr, Richard. *Everything Belongs: The Gift of Contemplative
Prayer.* Crossroad Publishing Company, 2003.

Rolheiser, Ronald. *The Shattered Lantern.* Crossroad, 1995.

Stabile, Suzanne. *The Path Between Us: An Enneagram Journey
to Healthy Relationships.* IVP Books, 2018.

Saint Augustine. *The Confessions of Saint Augustine.* Hackett
Publishing Company, 2006.

Benedict of Nursia. *The Rule of St. Benedict.* Vintage, 1998.

Thibodeaux, Mark E., SJ. *Reimagining the Ignatian Examen.*
Loyola Press, 2015.

Vanier, Jean. *Essential Writings*. Orbis Books, 2008.

Ware, Kallistos. *The Power of the Name*. Fairacres Publications, 1986.

Ware, Kallistos. *The Orthodox Way*. St. Vladimir's Seminary Press, 1995.

Wright, N.T. *The Meal Jesus Gave Us*. Westminster John Knox Press, 2015.

**Websites**

IgnatianSpirituality.com, a service of Loyola Press, https://www.ignatianspirituality.com/ignatian-prayer